Just Another Bloomin' Day!

Kandi Anderson

HOPE ADAMLEE PUBLISHING

Just Another Bloomin' Day!
Copyright © 2002 Kandi Anderson

Published by Hope Adamlee Publishing

Packaged by Pine Hill Graphics

Cover design by Brad Bullock

Publisher's Cataloging-in-Publication
(Provided by Quality Books, Inc.)

Anderson, Kandi,
    Are you buried under life's dirt and fertilizer? :
It's--just another bloomin' day : everyday reflections
and God's evidence in them / Kandi Anderson.
    p. cm.
    ISBN 0-9714103-9-9

    1. Christian life--Miscellanea. 2. Family.
3. Spiritual life--Christianity. I. Title. II. Title:
Just another bloomin' day

BV4501.2.A64 2002   248.4
               QBI33-864

Printed in the United States of America.

02 03 04 05 06 07 08 09 10 / 10 9 8 7 6 5 4 3 2 1

ACKNOWLEDGEMENTS

I thank you, Mama, for passing on the legacy of the language of love.

I thank you, Lowry, for being a husband who thinks his wife makes sense on paper, for encouraging me in this little adventure and for loving me thirty years into this gift called marriage. Thanks for making our lives fun, and certainly never dull!

My precious children, Melanie, Zach and Kasie, I know you're just glad that my rantings are on paper rather than being preached at you! I thank you for allowing me to write about my favorite people – you, your spouses, JJ (the encourager) and Tiffany (my friend), and the greatest joys of all, the girls – Lauren, Karlie, Sadie and Madison.

To my friend and boss, Roy, who trusted me enough without knowing me to sit behind a mic and talk about Jesus, and then after getting to know me, allowing me to continue, thanks!

To Debbie, my dearest friend, who listens faithfully every week to the story of the week, and who prays me on, bless you!

Morning Lite listeners, Morning Glory girls and Mixed Nuts, a special thanks to you who have laughed, listened and put up with me as I worked out a story on air, in a Bible Study or in a Sunday Morning devotion. You are my precious friends, my partners in prayer.

Thanks to the Sun Herald for allowing me to share with the readers of the Mississippi Gulf Coast, and to the readers for pulling up a chair every week and sharing a "moment" with me.

To Brad, the artist, to Pat, the editor, and to Rusty the paginator! To the Father Ryan House Bed and Breakfast and the Cornerstone Foundation for lettin' me stay to finish up!

You are all Gifts from God!

TABLE OF CONTENTS

Foreword

The pedestrian explained to the police officer dispatched to the scene that although he didn't see the vehicle that ran him over, he was positive it belonged to his mother-in-law. "Wait a minute," remarked the officer, "you said you were hit from behind. How can you be certain it was your mother-in-law?" The man said, "I recognized her laugh."

Kandi Anderson is my mother-in-law. She has absolutely ruined any opportunity for me to tell tacky mother-in-law jokes. I can't tell them in good conscience because Kandi is so bloomin' nice. She is one of the kindest, most thoughtful, caring, unselfish people I've ever known. If you poll her family, church members, co-workers, fans and friends, they'll concur that she fulfills her roles as wife, mother, grandmother and neighbor with a sweet spirit and a servant's heart. She is one of those people who, after spending a few minutes with her, you feel like you've known her all your life. She has the wonderful ability to make each person she meets feel loved and valuable.

Kandi is bubbly, bright and gifted as a broadcaster, speaker and writer. Many know her as an on-air personality at American Family Radio WAOY. Countless folks have been blessed by her newspaper articles in the Gulf Coast Sun Herald. Others have been inspired through her anointed teaching at churches, banquets and conferences. As a family member, I'm privileged to know Kandi behind the scenes. Out of the spotlight and away from the microphone, Kandi's faith is genuine, her love for others is real and her joy is authentic.

I could fill pages with compliments about Kandi's winsome ways and enthusiasm for life. However, what impresses me most is her love for God. Kandi is a sold-out, on-fire Christian. She has learned the secret of surrendering to the Lord and allowing Him to live His life through her. The key to Kandi's success is the life-changing, resurrection power of a Holy God. As she yields her life, He uses her in wonderful ways. Her goal in life is to glorify God. Kandi lives out the verse John 3:30, "He must increase, but I must decrease." (KJV)

During your lifetime you deserve to meet Kandi Anderson. If you spend a minute or a month with her, you will be encouraged, challenged and loved. As a humble servant she is quick to give God credit for all her blessings.

If you never meet Kandi face-to-face, then enjoy this book. It'll be the next best thing. Prepare to be blessed. I whole-heartedly endorse this inspiring book.

J. J. JASPER
Veteran Broadcaster/Author

God Bless you

LET'S SOW THE SEED

Don't worry when the enemy throws dirt at ya...
he's just losin' ground!

I truly believe that God wakens our senses to hear creation teaching us lessons, parables of praise. My children, when young, were the audience to my beliefs. They'd roll their eyes and tell others that I stayed a little too close to the microwave over the years. Bless their hearts, we'd be driving along and I'd start preaching. I could turn an, "I forgot my lunch" or "I made an A today" into a full-blown three point sermon.

Alas, my audience has grown up and left me, and now I find myself talking to a whole bunch of people about a whole bouquet of God's blessings – blessings that come up through the dirt and weeds of life. Yep, Monday through Friday, you'll find me at the radio station sittin' behind a microphone for an hour having my devotion time with a great group of people, the majority of whom I've never seen, but love.

Man, that is so amazing to me! I can run my mouth off and on for a whole sixty minutes and no one talks back!

With that blessing comes the tremendous responsibility of using that time well. I asked the Lord to teach me – He sent me to scripture, Isaiah 50:4 *"The Sovereign Lord has given me an instructed tongue, to know the word that sustains the weary. He wakens me morning by morning, wakens my ear to listen like one being taught."*

It's been my prayer to share a word that brings a little laughter and a word that sustains the weary. I've found that when I ask, God's always been constant in showing the wonder of Himself in life, and I just enjoy passing some of that love along. But there have been days when the ol' mind ain't what she used to be, and that's why I'm writing all the action down while it's still fresh. Another reason is therapy, y'all. Journaling the journey helps me remember what's popped up as I've ambled through the growing seasons of life, kind of like those empty flower-seed packages you see marking the planting at the end of the garden rows.

And honey, around my house we are always in a growing season. When you sow the seeds of "Lord, whatever you want, we'll do," your guess is as good as mine as what's going to sprout. We just know something's going to grow. It's like our preacher friend, Donny, told my husband, "Some days you feel like you're buried underground, don't ya? Well, break the dirt and bloom!"

I hope *you'll* come along as I walk through the dirt, the fertilizer, the sowing, the pruning and the harvest of a few of MY BLOOMIN' DAYS!

1
KNOWIN' THE GARDENER

FATHER'S VOICE

Deployment was a new word in our vocabulary, but it became defined in our lives when our son Zachary, a Marine, like many military men and women was scheduled to serve our country overseas. The days leading up to Zach's departure were filled with activity and unexpected phone messages. Yes, just prior to THE BIG DAY, my precocious granddaughter, Zach's niece, dialed up good ol' Unkie Zach in California. Not getting anything but the dreaded answering machine, Lauren proceeded to leave a recording of her own. Speaking directly and distinctly, there was no missing her point. She wanted Zach to quit his job. Lauren told Zach to phone his commander and tell him he couldn't go on board the ship. She hit hard with words like, "You can't leave your family. You will miss Karlie's first steps, her first birthday, her first Christmas. Unkie Zach you will miss too many firsts! You'll have to tell 'em you can't go!" Horrified, my daughter, Lauren's mom Mel, could be heard on tape screaming, "How did you get that number? Get off that phone! You can't do that to Zach!"

Zach got a good laugh from the ordeal. Tiffany, his wife, got the Message. With the gusto of a Marine spouse on a mission, she began to strategize and put in motion a plan that would allow Zach to remain a vital part of Karlie's life, even in his absence. Mom and dad wanted that sweet little girl to continue to laugh and smile when she heard her daddy's voice. They were determined that she remember him, to recognize him when he came home, to keep the relationship close. Quite a task since Karlie was a mere seven months old.

Movie tycoons had nothing on Tiff. On her command of lights, camera, action, the record of life began! The camcorder ran out of battery power many times as it captured Daddy reading Bible stories, strumming songs to Karlie on the guitar and playing games of peek-a-boo. Mission accomplished. Every day after the ship left port, the videos played. Karlie would giggle with glee as she watched her own personal movie of a Dad who loved her dearly. Just as hoped, when occasionally there was a call from another continent, she recognized and named that voice. Daddy was on the line and she knew it! That tiny face perked up as she would jabber into the receiver with the confidence of having close ties with the fellow on the other end. When he made it home, she knew beyond a shadow of a doubt that this was her father, her daddy.

Just like Karlie became acutely familiar with her daddy's voice, we need to be able to distinguish our Heavenly Father's voice from the many sounds that are filling the air. Making daily contact is a must. Listening to the passages that describe Him and the hope that He shares will lead us into relationship with Him. When there is personal relationship, He tells us, "My sheep know my voice."

There is security in that knowledge and there is joy. Karlie may not realize why her Daddy has to go far away, working to protect his family and her country, but she knows he loves her. Tiffany's efforts to keep a family close are paying dividends. Those same rewards can be yours. God is calling His sheep. He loves you. Can you hear Him?

❀ ❀ ❀ ❀ ❀ ❀ ❀ ❀

Breaking ground, y'all – Is your life full of noise? Mine sometimes is and everything seems to be calling my name! Do you take time every day to get away from the sounds of life to listen and learn, to hear and recognize the only voice that matters? Are you spending time in the Scriptures so that you might know Him better? Many things call for us to follow after them, please be sure to know His!

Blossoms from The Book – Isaiah 30:21 Whether you turn to the right or to the left, your ears will hear a voice behind you, saying, "This is the way; walk in it." *John 5:25* I tell you the truth, a time is coming and has now come when the dead will hear the voice of the Son of God and those who hear will live. *John 10:27* My sheep listen to my voice; I know them, and they follow me.

Petals of Petition – Father in Heaven, how wonderful it is that we can hear from You! Forgive us when we allow everything else to draw us away, to call us and to keep us from spending time with you. I thank you for the illustration that came from a little girl spending every day with a Daddy she couldn't see and remaining so familiar with his voice. Let us stay in Your Word that we might recognize the sound of our Savior. Help us not to be deceived by listening to anyone but You. May the truth of the scripture, "my sheep listen and follow" be fleshed out in our lives. In Jesus' name, Amen.

13

GIVING AWAY

Tyler woke up one Sunday morning with things other than church running through his mind. He stretched and came to the conclusion that his family should remain home. Yep, that's right, home fellowship was looking pretty good. It wasn't that Tyler didn't like going to church, but being eight years old and spotting a perfectly beautiful day, it just wasn't on his agenda. He presented his proposal to good ol' Dad. Oops, that was a miscalculation. Somehow omitting Sunday worship and Sunday school from the Pav family schedule was not an option.

Once at church, Tyler received more than he bargained for. He was given a precious picture of Christ's love. Here's how the Sunday-Go-To-Meetin' day played out. It just so happened that on this particular Sunday, there was a blood drive for a tiny premature baby named Hannah, who was born in weighing a whopping 2.9 pounds. She was doing well, but blood donations were needed. Her church family rallied around the blood donor van after church and went on in to share that life-giving commodity with one of their newest members.

One of those gathering at the Blood Mobile was Tyler's mom. Yep, Gail had stepped up to the plate, or rather the needle, and took the plunge. We all talked and laughed as she gave up her pint, drank her juice and left. Upon leaving the van and going to find her family in the church, she proceeded to become a limp noodle and pass out. Tyler crooked his head up to look at ol' Dad, and in a wizened voice drawled, "See, I told you we should have stayed home today."

Daddy Matt shook his head, collected himself, made sure his wife was getting adequate medical attention, peered down at his son and surprised us all by giving each of us a description that I'll never forget. He sat down by Tyler and shared a picture of Christ. He explained to Tyler that his mom got faint every time she donated blood, but even knowing that, she intentionally set out to do it anyway. This was her gift to baby Hannah, her expression of love. Having said that, he continued telling his son that this was, in a small way, similar to what Christ did for him. "Jesus knew He would suffer and die, but He chose, like your mama to give Himself as a gift that we might have eternal life. It was His love for us that held Him to the Cross and because Christ first loved us, we love Him. This is the reason we come to church to worship and to give back to the One who gave it all."

All part of a day in the life of a believer! It's adventure, learning and giving. It makes you want to rise and shine on a good Sunday morning and sing praises to His name. And you betcha, when the church doors open, Tyler and I are there!

❀ ❀ ❀ ❀ ❀ ❀ ❀ ❀

Breaking ground, y'all – I have always been so amazed by the love of the Father for you and me! That He chose to give up His live for us, that He accepted the humiliation, the ridicule, the desertion, the pain, and the excruciating death at the hands of the very people He was dying for, sinners. He knew the plan and stepped down from His place of authority in Heaven and went through that on my behalf, on yours. Why wouldn't I want to give all that I am on His behalf?

Blossoms from The Book – John 10:17-18a The reason my Father loves me is that I lay down my life – only to take it up again. No one takes it from me, but I lay it down of my own accord. *Philippians 2:5-11* Your attitude should be the same as that of Christ Jesus: Who, being in very nature God, did not consider equality with God something to be grasped, but made himself nothing, taking the very nature of a servant, being made in human likeness. And being found in appearance as a man, he humbled himself and became obedient to death – even death on a cross! Therefore God exalted him to the highest place and gave him the name that is above every name, that at the name of Jesus every knee should bow, in heaven and on earth and under the earth, and every tongue confess that Jesus Christ is Lord, to the glory of God the Father. *I Corinthians 15:10* But by the grace of God I am what I am, and his grace to me was not without effect.

Petals of Petition – Father, oh that You love us and You truly share everything with us, for us. Let us not waste a moment of that precious gift. Open our eyes to ways that we can in turn be Christ to others. Help us when we realize that our giving may not always be easy, but it is always best. How marvelous is Your tenderness, Your watch care, Your desire for us to be made complete in You, through Jesus. Help us to live today, so as to say clearly to the world that we are thankful and that His grace to us is not without effect!

HOP ON BOARD!

Memory milestones designate special times in the course of our lives. Like a mile marker on the road of life, one of those indicators cropped up for us when our son

Zach survived Marine boot camp and was graduating. Our family unit, dubbed either adventurous or nuts, decided that we would drive on over for the ceremony. Hey, it's only a mere thirty-one hours from the shores of Gulfport, MS to the beaches of San Diego, CA. We all liked each other, so we packed the ol' bags and tried not to dwell on the distance. Yep, this little jaunt would replace our dictionary's previous definition of "a family drive." Packed into a van were eight people ages 82 years young to three years old. Great grandma to great granddaughter, son-in-law to daughter-in-law-to-be, husbands and wives to sisters traveling from one side of the U.S. to the other to pick up a brother, a son, a grandson, an uncle, or a husband-to-be, depending on where you fell on the family tree. It was indeed an experience to be shared only by the stout hearted or foolish; we had both on board.

I'll never forget the morning we left as long as I live; neither will my backside! After praying up for the trip, the wheels on that van of plenty rotated forward to the tune of "From the Halls of Montezuma." All hands were saluting, faces somber and bodies rigidly at attention. We were on a mission. We were going to pick up a United States Marine! Onward Christian soldiers.

The motives behind this mode of travel were as varied as the occupants. It's amazing what compels us. Fear of flying, lack of funds, hunger for adventure, desire to miss school, loneliness, following the crowd or just being too young to have a say. But binding us all together in one common method of madness was our deep love and a desire to see our precious Zach. It didn't matter if you called him son, grandson, unkie Zach, brother, brother-in-law or fiancée, it was love that crammed us in for the ride.

This escapade of love had all the touches of life! In the

middle of it all was lots of laughter, a bit of down in the mouth syndrome, great expectations, moments of boredom, stretches of activity followed by suffering numbness, hunger, and satisfaction. But honey, there was absolute joy at the end of the journey. We made it together, basically different but the same. It was a great camera shot of a pack of people headin' toward heaven.

Now that's an excursion toward eternity! So pick up your passport, the saving grace of Jesus. Hitch a ride. It's a great adventure. You get to miss a hellish place. Your transportation is the finest, a chariot of faith. There's no lack of funds. Christ paid it all. Hop on board, there's a seat waitin' for ya! We're going to see the King!

❀ ❀ ❀ ❀ ❀ ❀ ❀ ❀

Breaking ground, y'all – Goodness, we ARE different, diverse in our backgrounds and race, but the Creator of us all is calling us to join Him. Along the way our worship styles may differ, our dress vary; yet, we are knit together in a common bond, the thread being our love for the Savior, a desire to see Him and to reside with Him forever on the shores of eternity. Oh, what a trip!

Blossoms from The Book – Colossians 2:2-3 …that their hearts may be encouraged, being knit together in love, and attaining to all riches of the full assurance of understanding, to the knowledge of the mystery of God, both of the Father and of Christ, in whom are hidden all the treasures of wisdom and knowledge.

Petals of Petition – Father, thank you for letting us ride with you. Help us to remember that though we are each uniquely made, we are intertwined by Your grace. May we honor you by finding joy in the trips – caring for and loving one another. And Lord, make us travel agents for you by showing others the Way. In Jesus' name, Amen.

TRADING FEARS

We're remodeling our home – therefore, my husband will travel. He's taking this opportunity to escape the confines of mess and check on his granddaughters. That's where a slight snag sneaks into the scenario. He had already visited all the granddaughters within driving distance and the only one he hadn't seen lives on the West Coast with our only son and his wife. The ol' boy had at best four days in which to complete his visit, and he doesn't fly. He has his own interpretation of the scripture, "Lo, I am with you alway." In his earthbound mind it reads, "**LOW**, I am with you alway!"

The odd thing is this trepidation of winged transportation relates to him only. He sure does encourage others to hop on board. In fact, I was one of the uplifted. I just recently returned from San Diego, having bitten the bullet and caught the big bird flying westward. As I was preparing to leave Gulfport and just before entering the secure area of the airport, Lowry patted my back, gave me a hug, increased the insurance and reassured me that there was absolutely nothing to fret about. I figure it's always easier to say to someone else that all is going to be fine. It's kind of like telling a fellow who's having a tooth pulled, it ain't no big deal. It's not, unless it's your pearly white that's being extracted.

So it's my guess that's why he didn't sleep for two weeks prior to, "Fasten your seat belts, we are preparing for take off." There was very little peace in my husband's heart. He had real anxiety concerning air travel. It just gave him the creeps and he would have rather had all his teeth pulled than fly.

We've talked about this phobia a lot. It's funny when you know a thing in your head is illogical, when you even teach classes about a thing called fear. You can quote scripture, "For God has not given us the spirit of fear, but of power, and of love, and of a sound mind." You can try to capture the apprehension that wells up inside you, but somehow it evades incarceration. We all have demons that we fight like that, but I am glad to say that I saw how the devilish thing could be overcome. We can have victory. I know – I have witnessed triumph.

The day of Lowry's departure was one I will always treasure in my heart. I watched the big guy, who was truly dreading the flight, as evidenced by the sweat balls on his forehead, walk through airport security to face fear head-on. He was able to do it, because he loved his son more than he feared the thing that would keep them apart. Yes, this picture of a man putting aside his own desire to stay on terra firma, to soar the skies and see a son was to me the brush strokes of how we are to love Christ.

Victory comes in being wrapped up in loving someone more than being gripped in the junk that holds us in bondage. We will not only be free to fly, but to soar the heights!

❀ ❀ ❀ ❀ ❀ ❀ ❀

Breaking ground, y'all – Is there something that's got you by the nape of the neck? Maybe for you it's something other than fear. It might be anger, resentment, just anything that keeps you from the One who loves you most.

Are you willing to ask the question, "Can I give this up? Am I willing to toss the stuff that trips me up and keeps me from the best? Do I love my Savior more?" Answering "yes" to that question can save a marriage, a job, a friendship, and a life. Loving God more, my friend, is where peace resides.

Blossoms from The Book – 1 John 4:16,18 ...and so we know and rely on the love God has for us. God is love. Whoever lives in love lives in God, and God in him. There is no fear in love. But perfect love drives out fear! *1 John 5:3-5* This is love for God: to obey His commands. And His commands are not burdensome, for everyone born of God overcomes the world. This is the victory that has overcome the world, even our faith. Who is it that overcomes the world? Only he who believes that Jesus is the Son of God!

Petals of Petition – Father, You are so much more important than anything this earth has to offer. Forgive me when I get stuck in thinking I can't do something because of fear. Forgive me when I don't want to let go of something because I enjoy it too much. Lord, You are far more valuable to me than all of that. Please give me the courage to shake off the chains that hold me earthbound, and thank You for the joy of loving You! In Jesus' name, Amen.

A FISHY STORY

Are you ready for a true fishy story? I'm going to cast the line back into the past. Here goes. Ziiiiinnnngggg – splash. Let's reel in this tale of fish who swam in a lovely simulated ocean environment. Their lot in life was to be aquarium dwellers. Not your average murky tank that cries out for an algae eater; no, this fish bowl was maintained to

21

the point of perfection. These denizens of the dime store had struck it rich. In our office we had a fish caretaker who took her job seriously. This tankologist made intricate daily checks to determine the health and welfare of these gilled creatures. A heater kept the water temperature perfectly suited to their sort, and the feedings were consistent and yummy. These little guys had it made in the shade.

They had no worries and absolutely no reason to hurry: no fishhooks teasing or tempting them with luscious worms or flies and no great sea predators waiting to make them lunch. They had a virtual playground of rocks, caverns, sea grass and filters. Their greatest cause for concern was the occasional curious visitor under 4 feet who would knock on or press a face to the glass. Other than that frightful vision of distorted lips, this school of fish had the ideal conditions and they thrived in their own little slice of heaven.

That is, until a large intruder ventured into the office. He was nineteen and sweaty. For some reason, unknown to any of us to this day, he had an urge to stick his hand into the depths of the tank. The fish must have been horrified, for surely at that moment, their perfect world became polluted. No aquarium manual could whip this fish bowl back into shape, the impeccability had been flawed, the balance breached. The fish met their doom.

I think of this story often, especially the time of year where the fields are alive with the bloom of spring, signaling the arrival of Easter. As beautiful as the scenery can be, it just ain't perfect. Man at one time had an ideal environment, straight from the Creator, but we goofed it up with our unclean disobedience. Food was ample and scrumptious. Creation's thermostat was designed to suit one and all. Man met and walked with God.

That is, until the hand of sin entered. Man began to die and his sin separated him from the Perfect. Yet, y'all, there is a manual that marks the way to enter once again into that place of perfection. God's Word tells us that He has made provision for our dirt to be removed. "Though our sins be as scarlet they will be as white as snow." We can come into that place of sparkling excellence – heaven, where no sorrow, no suffering, no tears remain. We can, because Jesus made a way. How? He died for us. "Therefore, if anyone is in Christ, he is a new creation, the old has gone, the new has come!" We are clean in Him. We have become fishers of men with a story to tell.

❈ ❈ ❈ ❈ ❈ ❈ ❈ ❈

Breaking ground, y'all – I sit here wondering how often we still make the same mistakes as Adam and Eve. We have a record of their mistakes. It should be easier for us as we have example after example of how damaging sin can be, and how it separates us from the One who loves us most. I don't know about you, but I just can't stand that separation. I am so thankful that He loved us while we were yet sinners and sent us Christ Jesus to bridge the distance, to set us free from the chains of death. O' Death where is thy sting, where is thy victory? We experience LIFE in Christ.

Blossoms from The Book – Isaiah 59:1-2a Surely the arm of the Lord is not too short to save, nor his ear too dull to hear. But your iniquities have separated you from your God. *Romans 5:8* But God demonstrates his own love for us in this: While we were still sinners, Christ died for us. *Romans 8:37-39* No, in all these things we are more than conquerors through him who loved us. For I am convinced that neither death nor life, neither angels nor demons, neither the present nor the future, nor any powers, neither height nor depth, nor anything else in all creation, will be able to separate us from the love of God that is in Christ Jesus our Lord.

Petals of Petition – Oh Lord God, how can we ever thank You enough for being long suffering toward us? What a rebellious and willful people we can be. You have given us such grace and mercy. Keep us aware of any actions that might displease You. If sin creeps back in, breaking our fellowship with You, chasten us and forgive us. Thank You for the provision You have made to redeem us fully and completely. We bless Your Holy name. May we reflect the Light of Christ in our lives as it is our joy to bring honor to Your name! In Jesus' name, Amen.

2

BREAKIN' GROUND

LEAP OF FAITH

I am here to tell y'all, grabbing any "sugar" from our oldest granddaughter, Lauren, can be a test of physical fitness. Our girl is a mover and a shaker. You've been around kids like her, poster children for the Energizer bunny. Well, on our last visit for a sugar fix, her bounce fell a few watts shy of a full charge. She had broken her arm in two places and wasn't quite up to snuff.

When I questioned Lauren about how she had gotten herself in this fix, she replied, "Field Trip." Yep, the ol' outing to the farm had been too much for this inquisitive, busy character. That bale of hay called her name, enticing the little monkey to shimmy up the straw, even though in plain sight a "No Climbing" sign warned of danger. I asked Lauren if she read the warning sign, to which she replied, "Mawmaw, that would be a minus." I believe that was code for NO, but her recounting of the event didn't end there. She rationalized the whole scenario with the words that have been uttered by many who have passed through the halls of childhood, "Well, Maxwell climbed up, so I did, too!"

Following suit will bite you every time, and it certainly

literally "cast" Miss Priss in a new role. She quickly found it was not a part she liked to play. No way, José! Normally adept and agile, Lauren had become a tad bit inept and fragile since it was her right arm she had put out of commission. She really didn't want to take any of this sitting down, but facts being what they were, she found that she often had to take a load off and ask for help.

That's where I entered the picture. After quickly snatching a kiss, Lauren lassoed me and begged me to be her cohort in crime. She desperately required a hand, a good right arm to assist her in donning some wild outfit. She needed me. I melted. I was ready to fix her dilemma. Herein lay the problem. She knew she had a need and that her Mawmaw could meet that need, but she was determined to call the shots.

When I reached out to dress her, she proceeded to explain to me exactly how to put her "get up" on over her cast. I mean she had it down to "roll up that sleeve, stretch it out – NO, THAT'S NOT HOW YOU DO IT." By golly, it was going to be her way or the highway! Boy, does that sound familiar. In fact, I think my granddaughter might have been genetically predisposed to be controlling in nature. "Ask" is a word seldom found in my vocabulary and "receive" isn't exactly my strong suit either. More than once, I've told the Creator of the Universe just how He could best extricate me from dire straits and then had trouble waiting for an answer, and just leaped in and did it my way. The outcome wasn't good, and what's more, the consequences weren't too great.

There you have it! Leapin' lessons from Lauren. Summed up in a single bound and wrapped up in plaster casts. Read and understand the signs. Jumping because Maxwell did can break a limb. When we are needy, it's best to ask for a hand, loosen our grip, let go and let God! Hey, that's a leap of faith that even Lauren could appreciate. Geronimo!

❀ ❀ ❀ ❀ ❀ ❀ ❀ ❀

Breaking ground, y'all – Have you ever been there? Let's just start at the beginning. SHE MISSED THE SIGN. How many signs do we miss every day? Have you followed the crowd and gotten yourself in a real pickle? Have you found that getting out of a jam requires some help? Personally speaking, I have lived all those little scenarios on too many occasions and found that I thought I was in charge of the fixin' only to find that I need to leave the mendin' and deliverin' to the Lord.

Blossoms from The Book – **Psalm 119:11** I have hidden your word in my heart that I might not sin against you. *Exodus 23:2* Do not follow the crowd in doing wrong. **Psalm 18:6,16** In my distress I called to the Lord; I cried to my God for help. He reached down from on high and took hold of me and he drew me out of deep waters.

Petals of Petition – Precious Lord, give us eyes to see the signs. Help us to hide Your word in our hearts, keep us ever vigilant and help us to follow after You. Father, let us walk in the fear of the Lord, not in the fear of man. Free us and loose us from the desire to be popular and the compulsive need to fit in; our significance is in You. Humble us that we might see our need for You Lord, to accept your way for our lives as the best way. Thank You, for You are in charge! Oh, that we'll call on You and know that we can trust you in and with everything. In Jesus' name, Amen.

OUT OF THE DUMPS

It was one of those days that just shouted, "Look out, if anything is going to go wrong, today is the day!" My boss had just left the country and the radio station where I work ceased to transmit radio waves. Need I say that silence is not golden in the ears of the radio listener? I could just see all these people with their faces twisted into a questioning grimace, ear up to the speakers, checking their dial. I changed into my superwoman cape and quickly got to work. I had a station to save!

Having determined that it was not an in-house problem, it became my job to head to the transmitter site, which is a "far piece" from the metropolitan area. Those towers are way, way out of civilization. The only things that might interfere with them and their transmissions would be a snake, wild animal or a nesting hawk. Ooooo, the thoughts that assailed my mind! The only other time I had been to the site was not a memory I'd like to share. Suffice it to say, it was an unplanned long walk in high chunky heels. My feet still have total recall. My husband had shared that joy with me, so I rang him up this time and asked him to make the journey with me. I told him every superwoman needs her superman to help her on life's wild adventures, but he wimped out with some poor excuse about having a job of his own and quickly suggested that I call a faithful friend.

What friend would lay down her own agenda and possibly her safety to go where only hunters and the things they hunt go? But my fearless buddy threw on her wonder woman cape and joined me for the trip. She was a great choice as these were her ol' stompin' grounds. We made it to the site, determined we couldn't fix the thing and called in the real heroes, engineers. As we made our way back home down winding, back roads, a funny thing happened.

Remember, my friend had grown up in "them thar woods," and she spied a familiar object from her childhood. It was a dumpster, y'all.

She starts hollering, "That's my dumpster spot! I've spent an afternoon in that thing." Who tells things like that? I started rolling with laughter as she shared the story. Her mama just knew that she had the winning number for the Publisher's Clearing House contest and it had been tossed into the trash. Ah, the proverbial quick fix to financial freedom. I've shared that pain, haven't you? The very thought sent this mama and her girl into a frenzy to find their ticket to wealth. Trash flew as the search was on but the winning numbers had flown the coop. I still get choked up thinking about my friend in the trash bin. What things are done in the name of the dollar!

We could laugh because the parties mentioned have all found that their treasures weren't going to be found in dumpsters. Yep, the trash bin didn't have the answer to life's problems. My friend discovered that when you look for hope in a pile of trash, you just end up smellin' like the stuff you're wallowing in. She has come to the realization that true wealth comes from something much more eternal and precious than money. This young lady has been richly blessed by trusting the Lord with her life. Hey, these days she's not stinking at all, but she's sporting the aroma of Christ. What a refreshing fragrance that is!

Wow, it might have begun a bad day, but I'm sure out of the dumps! Remember, God's got your number.

❀ ❀ ❀ ❀ ❀ ❀ ❀ ❀

Breaking ground, y'all – Goodness, our minds often tend to stray back to the dumpster; some people still live there.

31

Let's lift our hand and our eyes up and say Lord, "GET ME OUT OF HERE!" There is nothing good in the pits, it stinks and God does not redeem us for us to stay in the trashcan. We have the opportunity through the power of Almighty God to be lifted higher and to become the aroma of Christ, inside and out. Let's take it.

Blossoms from The Book – *Hebrews 9:14* How much more, then, will the blood of Christ, who through the eternal Spirit offered Himself unblemished to God, cleanse our consciences from acts that lead to death, so that we may serve the living God. *Philippians 3:13b-14* But one thing I do: Forgetting what is behind and straining toward what is ahead, I press on toward the goal to win the prize for which God has called me heavenward in Christ Jesus.

Petals of Petition – Oh Lord, we have been in the dung heap of shame and sin and You have washed us clean! How precious are Your thoughts toward us and how lovingly You restore us and lead us into green pastures. Help us to take captive those thoughts that would send us thinking that we deserve to remain in the trash piles. You have given each of us a measure of faith, a work to do and the ability through the loving, faithful power of the Holy Spirit to complete it! How much we love you, as you have rescued us from much! In Jesus' name, Amen.

POTHOLES AHEAD!

Wooooohhhhh! Splat. Ever felt like your life just hits one pothole after another? I've really been trying to avoid them myself. Now that's a tall order for such a deep subject. There are cavernous holes, ruts, gaps and disparities all over the place just waiting to catch you off guard. You must be vigilant and forewarned. Consider yourself by way of this missive, alerted. There's a pothole, somewhere, someplace, waiting for you when you least expect it, so just smile and join me in the pits.

I have been down roads notorious for catching a driver off guard, at night no less. There's a railroad crossing in Lumberton, MS, that's known for collecting exhaust pipes, transmissions and anything else that's slightly loose. I remember that hole; we met one evening, just bumping into one another slightly. But when I was asked to drive that way to speak again, I was on point. I knew that danger lurked on Highway 13 in Lumberton. Wisely my car slowed to a snail's pace, and gently greeted the rutted rails. I made it! No incident, or accident, I was free and clear of a would-be stumbling block.

Later that day I was minding my own business trying to get home in time to make banana pudding for guests that would be arriving. I went the back way, the shortest route. That could have been my first mistake. Stopped at a four way stop, greeted an oncoming car, spied a small saw-horse sitting slightly on the road. And that, my friend, was the only indication of anything amiss, which could have been my second mistake. I could tell the asphalt was being replaced, but there were no signs warning an unsuspecting motorist to "beware." Dubbed ol' fuddy duddy driver by my children, my foot is geared to stay at the understood "five miles" over the speed limit. So it was on this afternoon, I was on a slow steady pace when I was totally shocked to see "or not see" an extremely large differential in the road grade. Wow, just call me Daisy Duke! When my well-oiled machine hit that bridge change, I flew. For those of you who water-ski, this was like the ultimate ride over an extreme wake. My life passed before my eyes, I experienced weightlessness, but gravity called and I hit terra firma…hard.

Oh, you should have been there! I just knew my wheels had been pancaked and my axle sheared, but "thank you Lord," I made it home. I briefly told my husband a condensed version of the story, but skirting the details of the fiasco and thinking the car had survived could have been my third mistake. HA! The ol' saying, "your sins will find you out" proved to be all too true. Morning came and my omission of the "rest of the story" came. My husband had kissed me bye and was calmly playing with the dogs when I turned my car on, put it in reverse only to have sparks fly and the most awful grinding noise pierce the peaceful new day. Lowry was not a happy man.

Ah, the moral. Have you ever fallen in a pothole of sin? Have you been so far down in the mire of that cavern that the fall shook stuff loose, like your finances, your health, your joy? Did you finally confess it, get victory over it, thinking smugly, "I'll never hit bottom like that again?" Did you think you had a handle on the thing, forgetting to be vigilant and on guard? Did you, like me, put your life on cruise control? Once again, be warned! WATCH OUT, there IS a stumbling block with your name on it. Let's remember to say with the Psalmist, *"Show me the way I should go. Teach me to do your will, for you are my God; may your good Spirit lead us on LEVEL ground!"* Say it with me friends, LEVEL GROUND!

❀ ❀ ❀ ❀ ❀ ❀ ❀ ❀

Breaking ground, y'all – Sometimes, I'm just a slow learner and it takes a pothole or two to shake me up and get me back listening to the Teacher. My husband pointed out to me all the small warnings that hinted that I may be traveling down a dangerous road. Have you ever ignored telltale signs of danger? Have you ever disregarded Godly counsel? Have you ever hit bottom? Just because you didn't take the way of escape!

Blossoms from The Book – I Corinthians 10:13 No temptation has overtaken you except such as is common to man; but God is faithful, who will not allow you to be tempted beyond what you are able, but with the temptation will also make the way of escape, that you may be able to bear it. (NKJV) *Isaiah 40:4* Every valley shall be raised up, every mountain and hill made low; the rough ground shall become level, the rugged places a plain.

Petals of Petition – Father in Heaven, You stand watch over Your children, making provision for us. You know how often we need reminders that we are nearing trouble and You provide ways of escape. Please help us listen to the Holy Spirit and act correctly! Lord, thank You for rescuing us from the pit and setting our feet on the Rock. Thank You for teaching us, thank You for Your patience and thank You for the ability to choose to take the right roads and miss the caverns of sin. You are greatly to be praised! In Jesus' name, Amen.

GET A GLOVE ON IT!

It's never a pretty sight to watch someone who's lost her zing attempting to play a sport that requires some zip. You've probably heard it said, "It's best to quit in your prime, to go out a winner." Those words were probably whispered in the stands as onlookers gazed wide-eyed at my performance on the ball field, as I made my final bow to the game of church softball. Yep, that afternoon several years ago, I was a one-woman advertisement for gettin' while the gettin's good.

I can still hear Mrs. Shirley. All of you probably have known a Mrs. Shirley, softball's greatest fan, hollering at me from the sidelines as I made my way on the field. The powers that be had coerced me out of retirement because they were short a player and someone had snuck up and put my name on the roster. Promises were made about "only needing a body." Being church league softball, I didn't think the girls would be pulling my leg. Well, that wasn't all I pulled that day. Trouble started when I hit the ball over second base. It should have been a stand up double, but no, my legs turned into some foreign goulash and I found myself crawling to first base, where I begged for a runner.

It went downhill from there, literally. They put me on the pitcher's mound. Such a small hill, but as I went into my wind up, I wound up on the ground looking up at the sky. Hoots and hollers erupted from the stand and I was glad that I could provide all the elements for great entertainment: drama, slapstick, laughter and even a few tears. The latter fell from my husband's orbs when he thought I might actually be hurt and unable to whip up supper later that evening. Yet, the fiasco that blackened my career was still to come. I was thankful it wasn't my eye.

We were outfield and the consensus was to put me way out in right field. I kept praying fervently for the batter to hit in any direction but mine. I heard the crack of the ball and saw a blur of white cutting a path across the grass toward me. My mind shifted to an earlier time in my life when I could actually bend without cracking. My coach, Ellen Walker, used to expend endless energy telling me to get in front of the ball, bend down and stay with it. That's all fine and dandy when you're young. This was a different time and a different day.

With the ball rapidly approaching, and confidence being in short supply, I made a terrible miscalculation. I was fairly sure I knew where the play was to be made and I was almost positive I could get down in front of the ball. Here's the rub; I anticipated and made the play in my mind's eye before I actually had the ball in hand. I came up throwing air as the ball zipped past, only to be stopped by the fence. My, oh my, Ellen would not have been happy. I believe I could hear her voice ringing down the corridor of time, "Kandi, get the ball in your glove before you throw the thing!"

I don't know about you but that's been a hard lesson for me to learn in life. I often get ahead of God's timing, missing the play altogether. Are you with me here? Proverbs simply puts it, "It is not good to be hasty and miss the way." So, here's some good strategy from a softball retiree: "When life hits you a zinger, bend the knee to the Father, stay down 'til the situation is well in hand, and you won't drop the ball, but will make the play!" Batter up!

❀ ❀ ❀ ❀ ❀ ❀ ❀ ❀

Breaking ground, y'all – Okay, Let's talk. I don't think the question is "Have you ever?" No, I think the question is, if you are anything like me, "How many times have you run ahead of God?" Have you ever anticipated the next play on the field before it happened? Have you ever taken your eye off the game thinking that you had it all figured out? Have you ever quit listening for the coach's call because you had already decided that you could handle this one on your own? I have and oh, what a mess. I've missed the ball, fallen on my face and come up with a mouth full of mud! Oh, why don't we wait, watch, listen and work in tandem with the Father?

Blossoms from The Book – Proverbs 19:2 It is not good to have zeal without knowledge, nor to be hasty and miss the way. *Proverbs 19:21* Many are the plans in a man's heart, but it is the Lord's purpose that prevails. *Proverbs 20:25* It is a trap for a man to dedicate something rashly and only later to consider his vows. *Colossians 4:17* ...See to it that you complete the work you have received in the Lord.

Petals of Petition – Oh, Father, how many times have You patiently wiped the mud off my face? I am so thankful that You clean us up, forgive and set us back in the ballgame. Help us to run the bases, make the plays and finish the game listening to You for the calls. Please keep us from running ahead, from trying to do things all by ourselves and from not being a team player. Lord, You are so gracious and we praise You as You tenderly coach us through today! Thank you for calling us safe when we run home to You. In Jesus' name, Amen.

SOMETHING ABOUT THE NAME

Let me begin this missive by reminding you that this is being written by a woman named Kandi, daughter of King, married to Lowry, grandson of Elah, good names, all--- but not your average run of the mill, nor likely to be at the top of the best known, most popular list!

But there's just something about a name. Try living without one. They say my youngest granddaughter won't remember that she went home from the hospital, nameless. Ha, who are they fooling! With a big sister who takes after a grandmother who loves to share everything be it in print or in speech, the word's going to get out. So, 39546, the number on her identification bracelet will forever immortalize the newest addition to the family. Yep, that's what we called the bundle of joy from 9:20am on a Friday till the following Monday afternoon. Why? Mom and Dad were looking for a fit!

Names ARE important; just think how long you're stuck with them. There's that catchy, novel name that you're confident will set your precious one apart from all the rest. You never know just how far apart until you've seen one tested on the playground of life. It's always amazed me how a seemingly unimaginative group of kids, those who seem to have the most trouble in a simple English class, can come up with ways to rhyme a perfectly good given name with a dozen bad ones. Before labeling a newborn, we ought to run it by some of these wanna be bards. It might save a whole bunch of heartache.

Then there's the name that kind of grabs your attention until it rings a bell as you're transported back in time, remembering that "someone" whose attitude ruined it for all generations. It's been enlightening to see how easily a name is knocked off the list because someone tarnished the thing. There really is something to be said about guarding your name. On the same note, I've also noticed the smiles that suddenly appear on faces by the mere mention of a name, the name of someone you can trust, that you love, that you respect. A good name is worth a million.

Speaking of money, I'm beginning to believe that some of it's passed hands in our family over this name thing. Our ranks are swelling with granddaughters, and with each one the dilemma of attaching them with a brand of their own becomes stickier and stickier. It's been fun to watch our kids toss a name in the air and then fight with their siblings over who will get to use it in the future. I'm thinking it's costing someone. Once again a name is important. I never thought about it much until I was told how lonely it was not to be called by name. It's been said, "love is knowing that your name is safe in someone's mouth."

That wasn't the case for our son when he was in boot camp. In fact not being allowed to be called by his Christian name was a mental hurdle he had to learn to jump early on. An individualist who carries with him many nicknames, he will forever fit his given one, Zachary Adam. For sanity's sake he would lie in his bunk and say aloud, "Zachary Adam Anderson," over and over again so as not to forget that this was who he had been named. He said it helped to know that others were calling that name in prayer, but most important to him was the fact that his name was written in the Lamb's book of life and no man could change that truth. Jesus knew his name.

39546 now has a name. Her parents tried out many, again I say, many names on this new life and found one that seems to suit her personality, one that brings with it the promise of a fit. Madison Key Jasper is child that will make the name one to remember. A name that will be safe in our mouths, a name that will be continually held in prayer, a name that is shore 'nuff better than 39546. A good name is more desirable than great riches!

❀ ❀ ❀ ❀ ❀ ❀ ❀

Breaking ground, y'all – Have you ever studied the names of scripture? Each one bears an important meaning, and God has even changed people's names as their character

40

changes. Names are important. We didn't have much say in the names we were given, but we sure can keep that name safe by living Godly lives. By the same token, we can be very careful and selective when placing a name upon a child and we can keep that name safe in our mouths. But I am just thankful that God knows us by name!

Blossoms from The Book – Proverbs 22:1 A good name is more desirable than great riches; to be esteemed is better than silver or gold. *Luke 10:20b* …but rejoice that your names are written in heaven. *I Peter 3:15-17* But in your hearts set apart Christ as Lord. Always be prepared to give an answer to everyone who asks you to give the reason for the hope that you have. But do this with gentleness and respect, keeping a clear conscience, so that those who speak maliciously against your good behavior in Christ may be ashamed of their slander. It is better, if it is God's will, to suffer for doing good than for doing evil. *John 10:3-4* The watchman opens the gate for him, and the sheep listen to his voice. He calls his own sheep by name and leads them out. When he has brought out all his own, he goes on ahead of them, and his sheep follow him because they know his voice.

Petals of Petition – Father, Praise Your name! That Name that is above all names! How marvelous is Your grace to allow us to have our name written in the Lamb's book of life. Lord, keep us from slandering one another and harming another person's good name. Help us to guard our names this side of heaven so that when others hear ours mentioned, they will think of You. In Jesus' name, Amen.

3

SOWIN' SEED

THIS LITTLE PIGGY PICKS A MARKET

What's up with the market? Nothing. That's not funny, is it? We've been funding the ol' piggy bank for years only to find that when the little piggy went to market, it got lost. The steak we hoped to buy turned to roast beef, then we found we could afford none and now it's got some of us crying all the way home. I've realized that life has its ups and downs and if we trust our joy to things like markets, piggy banks and pension funds, the anti-acid makers are going to be the winners. I know I get queasy just thinking about the world of stocks and bonds. I'm clueless when it comes to portfolios and the like.

So if I don't understand anything about keeping up with the Dow or the Jones, why am I even trying to write about the subject? I'm going to attempt to share with you about investing. That's right. Since that's a by-word in today's world, I would like to try my hand at being an investment analyst. Invest has synonyms like put in, spend, devote, advance and deposit. Those words all have the sound of costing us something, things that we can be stingy with like our money, our time, and our comfort. And the way the market's been acting we better find an account that has value.

I'm no stock picker, but may I make a suggestion? The ol' Family Fund. It means investing our time, our thoughts, our prayers, our hopes, and our money. How can we demand withdrawals of trust, respect and obedience if we haven't made any deposits? I'm telling you, this one fund will put a kink in our pocketbooks, our agendas, and our energies, but if we fail to credit the above assets into our family's tally, it will flat-out knock a hole in what's important and lasting and eternal.

It seems like yesterday that our children were small and we were investing. Now my babies are putting their hearts into their children. In fact, my son-in-law brought it home when he said, "Gosh, Melanie really understands our girls. She's such a good mom. The detailed list that she left for the sitter when we were on the way to the hospital to have baby number three gave the times for meals, for naps, for mood swings and the guttural sounds for each." Melanie knows her children because she's fully vested in motherhood.

Being vested means giving time and often the hardest commodity to come by is time. But it can be done. I have a CPA friend who is swamped during tax season, but still makes ballgames and school activities. How? He sacrifices. He's on the job at four in the morning and then hits the books after the kids are in bed. He knows which accounts are worth more per hour and pay the highest dividends.

The growth in our family investment will sometimes appear as volatile as an out of control market. The teenage years sometimes find the fund plunging, but that's the very moment we need to sacrificially add to the account, for tomorrow we will reap what we have sown. So many times I have missed opportunities to invest. I put my assets in other people's funds and lost dividends, so my investing motto is this, y'all: I will not give to others what I have not first given at home!

Let's end this trip to the market with a word from the Proverbs, "Cast but a glance at riches, and they are gone, for they will surely sprout wings and fly off to the sky like an eagle." For that reason this ol gal's little piggy bank is in the treasury of home.

❀ ❀ ❀ ❀ ❀ ❀ ❀ ❀

Breaking ground, y'all – I don't know about you, but this thing with 401(k)'s going south has a bunch of my friends and me thinking on what's truly important. Do you know where your treasure is? Where's your heart? A lot of us were sure that money was the least on our list, until the market started doing a flop. Have you been seized by the world system and, after asking the Lord to "search you and show you if there was any wicked way in you," realized it had a bigger hold on you than you thought? Understanding comes quickly when our world starts changing. Family, home, friends, and most importantly a PERSONAL RE-LATIONSHIP WITH THE SAVIOR, these should be primary. Remember, Faith, Hope, Love remain.

Blossoms from The Book – *Proverbs 15:6* The house of the righteous contains great treasure, but the income of the wicked brings them trouble. *Proverbs 24:3-4* By wisdom a house is built, and through understanding it is established; through knowledge its rooms are filled with rare and beautiful treasures. *Matthew 6:19-21* Do not store up for yourselves treasures on earth, where moth and rust destroy, and where thieves break in and steal. But store up for yourselves treasures in heaven, where moth and rust do not destroy, and where thieves do not break in and steal. For where your treasure is, there your heart will be also.

Petals of Petition – Oh Father, You are everlasting and Your promises endure forever. I am so thankful for that! We ask Your forgiveness when our eyes get off the truth that what You hold dear is different from what the world holds dear. We ask you to forgive us when we join the trends of the world, looking to the dollar for security. What a lasting treasury you have given us in loving You, our families, our church family and friends. Help us to invest wisely today. Be honored by our decisions. In Jesus' name, Amen.

WIELDING THE WEAPONS

Ants. De dum, de dum, de dum. Can't you just hear the lead ant beating out cadence as the army of pesky critters marches in from everywhere and nowhere! I've been told by reliable sources that these invasions are taking place enmasse in many of your homes. The knowledge that I'm not the only one being assaulted by ants should make me feel better, but it's not taking the bite out of the fact that these ants are causing me considerable distress. They are marching in at alarming rates. It's so exasperating. There's no telling where their point of entry is, and they are biting me when and where I least expect it.

Why they're even following me to work. I walked in one morning to find these tiny creatures working up a sweat, dancing a jig on my desk. They didn't seem disturbed at all by my outrage, nor were they intimidated by my size. They seemed to think they were in control. I was about to show them just who was boss, that size DID matter and if that didn't get their attention, then maybe the can of bug spray would! I proceeded to the next room to locate the liquid exterminator. Lo and behold there stood the can of ant spray, but it took me a minute to realize it because the label wasn't legible. It was covered in ants! They were crawling up and down the big, bad terrible can unaware that it was the likely source of their demise. They showed absolutely NO FEAR.

Now, I know that bug spray works. I've used it with success. The commercials are true. It lives up to its claims. You just have to point and shoot. The little nuisances should have been trembling, but they weren't acting concerned because the can of "ANT AWAY" wasn't in use. It was dormant on the desk. It wasn't until I picked up my weapon of choice and swiped at the black lines being drawn by those bugs that they scrambled. When I put my arsenal to work, the war was quickly won!

Blow the trumpet! Sound the alarm! We have been given everything we need to fight the fight of faith! Scripture and the other weapons of our spiritual warfare are like that can of bug spray. THEY have the power of bringing down the strongholds, the buggers of life; but the debuggers have to be pressed into service. We have to do our part!!! The battle is not going to be won by wringing our hands, or by having the Bible sitting next to us, praying that we will get the message by osmosis. We must press them into service and we have to be vigilant and active members of the ARMY OF GOD.

Sweet victory. OH, NO! I didn't say "sweet." HERE THEY COME AGAIN!!!!

PUT ON THE ARMOR AND BRING OUT THE ARSENAL!

❧ ❧ ❧ ❧ ❧ ❧ ❧ ❧

Breaking ground, y'all – Have you ever felt defenseless? Have you looked around only to see the enemy surrounding you, coming in from you don't know where and then having the audacity to take a pound of flesh at will? It seems that the world is cocky and those trying to live in it as children of God feel like we are the underdog. Have we forgotten that our Lord has OVERCOME THE WORLD? Has it slipped our minds that we are given everything we need, but we have to make every effort to put on the armor and use the weapons we've been given?

Blossoms from The Book – *II Peter 1:3-7* His divine power has given us everything we need for life and godliness through our knowledge of him who called us by his own glory and goodness. Through these he has given us his very great and precious promises, so that through them you may participate in the divine nature and escape the corruption in the world caused by evil desires. For this very reason, make every effort to add to your faith goodness; and to goodness, knowledge; and to knowledge, self-control; and to self-control, perseverance; and to perseverance, godliness; and to godliness, brotherly kindness; and to brotherly kindness, love. *Ephesians 6:10-11* Finally, be strong in the Lord and in his mighty power. Put on the full armor of God so that you can take your stand against the devil's schemes.

Petals of Petition – Precious Father, oh, how wonderful Your Word is to me! Oh, that we are given everything, not just some of what we need to make it through today. We don't have to be wimps, or afraid, or weak. Just renew our minds and help us through the Holy Spirit to remember to put on the Armor, to make the effort to do what You have laid out for us in scripture. What power is ours, what strength, what wisdom, what grace for today. Thank you, Lord. In Jesus' name, Amen.

PUSH UP – HERE I COME!

The simple pleases. Let me say that again a little differently. The simple things in life bring joy. Wish I had known that before I made my Christmas list! Wouldn't you think it would be the elaborate do-dads, the latest fads, and the most expensive item on the shelf that would bless someone's socks off? Well, that's what I would have guessed, but boy, was I shown a new slant on that one! Yep, once again, a little child has helped me see the light.

When our granddaughter Lauren was five, she and her mom and dad were heading to Kentucky for a continuation of their Christmas season. Along the Natchez trace, Dad stopped at a gas station and as he went in to pay, he thought about getting Lauren her favorite goodie, an Orange Push-up. Wouldn't you know it, the store was out of this particular goody, but there was a different kind of Push-up, a rainbow-colored one. It would have to do. When daddy JJ handed this new fangled Popsicle to Lauren, she thankfully grabbed it. There was, just for a moment, a trace of disappointment on her face, only to be replaced by a look of wonder and a drool of anticipation as she quickly prepared to lick this multi-colored treat.

Lauren was so taken with this new Push-up she wanted everyone to give it a taste. Hey, this was a hit! So Daddy, upon noticing her enthusiastic response, realized this had just elevated him to the status of "Dad is Great!" Thinking that he could rake in a few more points, he told Lauren that on the way back home from Kentucky he would stop at the same store and buy her another Push-up just like the one she was slurping down. Lauren was so preoccupied with getting every last drip of the Push-up in her mouth that she didn't respond. It seemed that the episode was forgotten.

Once in Kentucky, the family was out building a snowman before opening gifts, when out of the blue, Lauren, hands on hips, pronounced emphatically, "Okay, I'm ready to leave!" The whole group was pretty astonished at this abrupt announcement. Piled inside the house were gifts galore waiting to be opened and Lauren was ready to go home? Had she momentarily lost her mind? What was the deal? Her answer was an emphatic, "Those Push-ups were so good, they'll probably be sold out if we don't get there quick."

With all the wonderful presents that awaited her pleasure that day, Lauren was longing for the unpretentious taste of Push-up! Their visit complete, the family bundled up and turned their car toward home. An expectant and persistent voice kept asking, "How much longer? How much longer?" Finally, when an exasperated mom said, "About thirty minutes," Lauren's face lit up with a grin and she threw her arms in the air and hollered, "PUSH-UP, HERE I COME!"

When they finally made it to the gas station, Daddy thrilled this darlin' even further by purchasing a bunch of those rainbow Push-up popsicles. Satisfied with the simple, they merrily went on their way.

I laughed with joy as they recounted this story. I was reminded that this mirrored my life in Christ. Having once "tasted" and having been overwhelmed with satisfaction that comes from the Savior, I want to know Him more. I am constantly hungering to move from the busyness of life and all it has to offer to the simple pleasure of spending time with my God. Here is the additional joy. When I hunger and thirst for His righteousness, when I seek Him with all my heart, I find that He has been waiting to give me "exceedingly, abundantly more than I could ever think or ask for! LORD, HERE I COME! I simply long for You.

❀ ❀ ❀ ❀ ❀ ❀ ❀ ❀

Breaking ground, y'all – When was the last time you hungered for the wonder of God? When was the last time you just couldn't wait to spend time with the Father? When was the last time you realized the simplest and most precious pleasures are found at the feet of Jesus?

Blossoms from The Book – *Psalm 34:8* Taste and see that the Lord God is good! *Psalm 119:103* How sweet are your words to my taste, sweeter than honey to my mouth! *I Peter 2:1-3* Therefore, rid yourselves of all malice and all deceit, hypocrisy, envy, and slander of every kind. Like newborn babies, crave pure spiritual milk, so that by it you may grow up in your salvation, now that you have tasted that the Lord is good.

Petals of Petition –Oh Father, how simply wonderful You are! The glitter and glitz of this world have nothing to compare with the joy found purely in spending time with You! Take away any taste we might have for the things that are wrong in our lives, the sins that ruin our spiritual taste buds, and help us to hunger for You. Thank You for all the small ways You show Your complete love for each of us! Oh Lord, having enjoyed that fellowship, having tasted and seen that You are good, how could anything else compare? Keep the wonder, the eagerness and the delight in being Your child always in the front of our minds. In Jesus' name, Amen.

CATCHIN' ON!

Do you catch on quick? Do you retain lessons that hooked you in the past? My husband and I have been married so long that I'm surprised my fragile memory even recalls the earlier events in our journey together, but some things you learn quickly and some things you never forget! Let me tell you about the time I got "schooled" in the things to clean in a fellow's life.

Every now and then I get an urge to spruce up everything in sight. In the newer days of our marriage we didn't have a whole lot to tidy up, but my husband did have a tackle box and it was mighty messy. Hanging out from the closed lid were wisps of fishing line and, when opened, there were nasty worms of various colors looking as if they had lost their wiggle. Nothing was organized and a bunch of the stuff in there appeared old and worn out, so I knew my new husband would love me more if I cleaned and organized his tackle box. With that thought in mind, I got with it! Anything that smelled too fishy was tossed. All of the older spoon-looking thingamadoodles went straight into the trash. Why would anyone want to keep hooks with three sides, hooks that were so small, or little round "bb" looking pieces of lead? Just thinking about how pleased my big fisherman was going to be when he got home made my task easier and the barbs a little less painful.

Ladies and Gentlemen: News Flash, a Blast from the Past. You do NOT touch the sacred, and that honey, would be the contents of the Fisherman's jewelry box. Nope, the barbs on the fishing hook weren't nearly as painful as the shocked and cloudy look I received from my husband when he saw how helpful I had been. In my opinion, he should have been beaming with joy and overflowing with words of love. Instead he became a madman, frantically rummaging through the trashcan!

I began to reflect on that day in time and realized there are some things we can't clean up for another person. Bringing attention to his need to tidy up might have been a better course of action. I believe it might be called Communication 101, in the school of marriage. I suppose God used this experience to teach me that there are quite a few things in our lives that aren't in our area of fixin' and cleanin'! Oh, I know that sometimes we want to be helpful and "clean" up our spouses, our friends and family. Next time you catch yourself trying to arrange someone else's spiritual life and schedule, remember only that person can choose to change his current state of messy. Some things are just hands off and better left to the Savior and your loved one.

Well, it's been almost three decades since my faux paux, when my fishy got fried and I learned one of the best lessons ever. Love the fisherman, keep your own tackle fresh, organized and intact, pray for good fishing, and let the Holy Spirit hook, reel in and clean the fish and the fisherman. He sure did a fine job on my salty dog, and these days his tackle box is looking goooood!

❀ ❀ ❀ ❀ ❀ ❀ ❀ ❀

Breaking ground, y'all – Are you a fixer? Have you ever tried to "save" someone by putting tracts under their coffee cup, telling them how they would be better if they just did it this way, or by pointing out all their faults? Boy, I have. God showed me early on that I was not my husband's

Holy Spirit. Nope, the Lord does a much better job. He also has taught me that I can't rescue everyone. That when I try to clean up for someone else, it takes longer for that person to learn what God is trying to teach them. Once again, God's timing, His improving work is best and it's the only clean-up that lasts.

Blossoms from The Book – Ezekiel 36:25-27 I will sprinkle clean water on you, and you will be clean; I will cleanse you from all your impurities and from all your idols. I will give you a new heart and put a new spirit in you; I will remove from you your heart of stone and give you a heart of flesh. And I will put my Spirit in you and move you to follow my decrees and be careful to keep my laws.

Petals of Petition – Father, forgive me when I try to run someone else's life. Remind me Lord, that every time I step in to "fix" someone, it's like I don't trust You or I'm in too big of a hurry for the results. Please teach me patience and give me more faith to allow You to complete the work that You have begun in each of us. I praise You, Lord, for I have seen Your mighty hand work to save and to save COM-PLETELY. I am expectantly waiting and knowing that You are working out in each of us Your grace. In Jesus name, Amen.

LET IT RIP!

I was feverishly wrapping up a week at work when the telephone rang. Communication was nearly impossible. It was the dreaded "can you hear me now?" kind of connection. The only thing clear about the reception was that this call was intentionally fuzzy.

The fragmented conversation went something like this, "Have appointment with Mr. And Mrs. Green…krrrrkkk.

Tony's coming along to clear the fairway...krrrk. Dropping his children ... krrrkkk ... by the house. Will be home after dark ... krrrkk."

Now, I wasn't born yesterday. Mr. Green and Mrs. Green have received more counseling than any couple known to man, as my Daddy had in the past counseled them every Wednesday and Saturday. Plainly speaking, it was the golf course beckoning my husband and our youth pastor, and I had just been appointed to spend some quality time with Tony's children, Kayla and Colton. This clearly was not what I had expected to be doing on a Friday evening, but I'm going to be real honest here: I was excited. It meant that I could kick back and become a kid again. I could chunk the paperwork, the laundry and the big person junk. I could fly on my bike!

It's likely Kayla and Colton found all the stuff we packed in those couple of hours normal, but for me it was far from routine.

After riding our bikes, picking up frogs the size of our thumbnails, tossing dog food to the fish in the pond, doing the limbo, playing badminton, and exploring the attic, we stopped to catch our breath. Standing by the pond we heard a new sound...knock, knock, knock. Our heads popped in the direction of the tapping and I whispered with a finger to my lips, "shhhhh, did you hear that?" Kayla and Colton bobbed their heads up and down as big breathy "yeahs" came from their mouths. Giggles leaked out as we tiptoed like safari hunters to find the source of the knocks. Standing at the base of a sawed-off dead tree, we heard the continual rat-a-tat-tat of a woodpecker's beak. We hollered for Mr. Woodpecker to come out and play and, lo and behold, the feathered knocker took a peek at us through a hole in the tree. Laughter rolled across the yard.

Now that's living! Give it a whirl. Cruise back in time on a bike, hike in the woods, and listen with an expectant ear. Delight in, drink in and just get delirious as you actually enjoy God's creation. You can do it! I promise I won't tell. I know your pressed and polished demeanor might be momentarily shattered, but break loose and let 'er rip. Christ said we must become like little children, so go ahead and shout to the heavens with childlike abandon, with joy.

Don't worry, the real world returns quickly enough. The heavy robes of responsibility will soon fall back on the ol' shoulders, but they may fit better and feel a smidgen lighter for having spent some time having a blast.

Thanks Kayla. Thanks, Colton. Thanks, God. My week ended on a high note. Yours can, too. Enjoy.

❀ ❀ ❀ ❀ ❀ ❀ ❀ ❀

Breaking ground, y'all – Goodness, there is nothing like spending time with a child to bring the kid out in us! We need to toss the heavy garments of responsibility and remember there is importance in enjoying God's creation. How often have you looked over your shoulder to make sure no one was watching when you decided to take a moment to relax? It's like we are in a contest to see who has the most to do and who is carrying the heaviest load. I'm here to tell you that I am glad two little children led me to the joy of just having fun!

Blossoms from The Book – *I Chronicles 29:28* He died at a good old age, having enjoyed long life, wealth and honor. His son Solomon succeeded him as king. *I Timothy 6:17b* …but to put their hope in God, who richly provides us with everything for our enjoyment. *Proverbs 17:22* A cheerful heart is good medicine, but a crushed spirit dries up the bones.

Petals of Petition – Oh, Father some days I feel like an old prune. Dried and shriveled up from all the "important" things I have wrapped myself in. Help me to remember it's not by works that we are saved. I get mixed up sometimes and forget how to laugh, and to play, remind us that it is all right to enjoy this life. Thank You for children who seem to automatically know how to abandon themselves to take pleasure in the wonderful creation You have shared with your people. Give us balance today, Lord. Bless those who are burdened today, and Lord help us to remember that "Your yoke is easy and Your burden is light!" Your love is extravagant, and greatly are You to be praised. In Jesus' name, Amen.

4
FERTILIZIN' DIRT

OLD AS DIRT

Psalm 37 has a verse that reads, "I was young and now I am old…" Like I needed a reminder of that fact. As another birthday rolls around, who needs a prompt on that subject? It seems like yesterday I was trying to RUSH tomorrow. Now I'm trying to JUMP BACK into yesterday or at least HOLD ON to today!

For women and for the honest guy, aging has a colossal impact on a thing called vanity. Can you recall the first time that young whippersnapper called you "ma'am" or "sir?" If you haven't heard it yet, you will. I'm here to tell you it's a crummy reality check when someone besides you notices the wrinkles and tells you about them. Often your first brush with the confirmation of what you've been noticing in the mirror will come from the innocent banter of an honest child.

May I share my experience? Josh was four at the time and his big brother Brock was six – two young men, intelligent beyond their years. They happened to be observing some of us gals at church as we were putting together welcome baskets for new members. Josh said, very matter-of-factly to his brother, "Time flies!" Brock replied, "Yep, that's right. We've been in school 158 days." Josh repeated, "Time flies." I broke in with a bit of elderly wisdom, "Especially as you get older." Then came the blow to the ego as Brock looked directly at me and said, "It must be flying really fast for you."

Wow, what a wallop, what a near k-o! I was sharing this with a friend when he said he could go one better. WARNING: The following is a true story. This particular friend, we will call him Bill, headed on a mission to the local Social Security office. He had come of age. It was time to fill out the forms necessary to receive funding for his longevity, the Social Security check. This was not one of Bill's happier days. His arrival at the building that housed the governmental institution found him with his head bent, heavy with solemnity of the moment. Bill never lifted his eyes even as the doors of the elevator opened to his floor. As he attempted to disembark, out of the corner of his eye he caught sight of a gray-headed ol' geezer with a mustache. He kept doing the boot scoot shuffle, trying to get out of the fellow's way. It got ridiculous, something straight out of a Lucille Ball skit. Finally, totally frustrated, he glanced up to say EXCUUUUSE ME, when he was faced with the reality of his own reflection. You guessed it! The elevator doors opened to reveal a mirrored wall. Ol' Bill had been battling his own image, one a whole lot older than he had previously thought. What a bummer!

Birthdays stacking up? May our eyes pop open to the fact that "time is flying," but we have a purpose and we serve a God who desires to direct our paths—One who loves us and will never leave or forsake us in our old age.

Hallelujah. And If your mind is still capable of holding a thought, maybe you'll remember we started this story in Psalm 37 with a verse that begins with a wake-up call of its own and ends with a promise for God's children, a gift for the aged and aging…."I was young and now I am old, yet I have never seen the righteous forsaken or their children begging for bread."

❀ ❀ ❀ ❀ ❀ ❀ ❀ ❀

Breaking ground, y'all – So what's the point? Every day is precious. Don't make it go faster than it should by rushing through life. If we are to give an account for every idle word, what are we going to do about all those misspent moments? From this second on we need to hold every one of those fleeting gifts up to the light of eternity and be fully living in that Light every hour, regardless of our age. God has given to each of us a calling. The Apostle Paul urges us in scripture to live a life worthy of the calling we have received. A noted pastor, let's call him Tommy, puts it this way, "Participate fully for Christ in your vocation on location."

Blossoms from The Book – Psalm 90:12-17 Teach us to number our days aright, that we may gain a heart of wisdom. Relent, O LORD! How long will it be? Satisfy us in the morning with your unfailing love, that we may sing for joy and be glad all our days. Make us glad for as many days as you have afflicted us, for as many years as we have seen trouble. May your deeds be shown to your servants, your splendor to their children. May the favor of the Lord our God rest upon us; establish the work of our Hands for us. Yes, establish the work of our hands.

Petals of Petition – Father, Maker of heaven of earth and of me! Thank you for the days you have given me. Forgive me when I rush through them without stopping to seek your plan for the minutes. I get buried, Lord, under piles of stuff and feel like I can't breathe. Breathe on me, Lord. Renew the spring in my step and help me as I age to grow in wisdom and in faith and in love and in the doing of all of these. Number my days and help me to bloom in the passing of the moments for Your glory. In Jesus' name, Amen.

MICROWAVE MADNESS

Cold? Did someone say cold? I don't know if that description is strong enough for what I felt that day. You got it. I was an absolute cube. It must have been the coldest day of the predicted freeze days. The sun hadn't been doing its thing very long, but it sure didn't look that cold. My friends, looks can be deceiving. The windshield seemed to have only a thin glaze of ice. No problem, I had carried a bowl of water to pour over the glass to clear up that little frosty snag. WRONG! All that did was increase the density of the ice. This called for some cold weather equipment. Now, I am a Southern girl. We used to shut down the schools when the temperature dipped into the high 30's, so do you think my car was equipped with an ice scraper? Nope. Gloveless, I had to scrape the windshield with a CD cover.

Visibility insured, I proceeded to take my frozen self to work. Now, just to draw you the picture, the building I work in is an old wooden structure set up on blocks. It is nippy in there on a mildly cold day. Today my eyebrows started accumulating ice and my hands felt like they were on the verge of a good case of frostbite. I needed a quick warm up. Always flexible, I spied a pair of socks that had doubled as gloves for me earlier in the week. I picked them up and put them on. They were glacial. This was no hill for a stepper. A friend had shared with me the handy trick of putting a dishrag or sponge in the microwave to kill the germs, so my frozen brain begin to spin the problem around and I thought, quick fix. MICROWAVE. SOCKS. Hhmmm. HEAT. Ta da! Oh, you are good. Yes, I did do it. I threw them in the ol' micro and turned up the juice and shivering, went back to work.

It wasn't long until my nose hairs began to curl. There was definitely something "in the air" and it wasn't good. The guys had just rewired the building the day before so I assumed it was just that new electrical burn off kind of smell. WRONG. I followed the curling smoke into the area that housed the microwave. The unusual aroma had taken on a life form and was visibly pouring out of the door of that appliance. I opened it to find the remnants of my thick socks, smoldering. Oh, my goodness. I took those babies and tossed the evidence of my foolishness in the trashcan. WRONG. Remember what the cookbooks say about food continuing to cook after microwave removal. Ditto.

The wastebasket began smoking. Problem solver that I am, I took the offensive remains of my socks and tossed them on the concrete steps outside. WRONG.

At that time I didn't realize how wrong. Upon re-entering the office I found it difficult to breathe. The smoke was heavy. My frozen state was going to last a little longer because all windows and doors were going to have to be opened. I was praying for a quick clearing as my boss would be in soon and I sure didn't want to explain this one. Tossing open the back door to get a good draft going, I found that the cold air blowing outside had ignited my socks, y'all. They were flaming, and the conflagration was licking at the wooden structure. I think it was at about this point that my brain began to thaw. I doused those socks with a couple of glasses of water. Finis'. The socks were soot.

Other than a new understanding of fire safety, what's the message in all of this? A friend put it this way, "I sure have started a lot of fires in my life which the wind has fueled. Now with God's grace those wild fires are out." HEY! THAT'S A THOUGHT THAT THAWS!!!!

❀ ❀ ❀ ❀ ❀ ❀ ❀ ❀

Breaking ground, y'all – I'm looking at it like this, do you ever get the urge to get comfortable quick? Impulsive moves to fix it. Not asking God. Don't want to bother Him, "I'll do it MYSELF" comes to mind. That reckless discipline has started many a wild fire! Once ignited, smoke rises. Then we attempt to extricate the fuel from the inferno, but the smoldering continues. All it takes is the wind blowing the right direction to fan the embers into flames again. Before our lives become "soot" we need to douse them in a good soaking of God's grace, wisdom and timing. That's a good heart warmer and true flame extinguisher.

Blossoms from The Book – Isaiah 50:10-11 Who among you fears the Lord and obeys the word of his servant? Let him who walks in the dark, who has no light, trust in the name of the Lord, and rely on his God. But now, all you who light fires and provide yourselves with flaming torches, go, walk in the light of your fires and of the torches you have set ablaze. This is what you shall receive from my hand: You will lie down in torment.

Petals of Petition – Creator of Heaven and Earth, why do we always try to take matters into our own hands? Forgive us. Teach us to wait. To seek Your design and to remember when we are uncomfortable, our ways are not always the best way to ease our discomfort. But You, Oh Lord, choose to teach us in the midst of our hardships. Help us to walk in Your Light and warm us by that Light! In Jesus' name, Amen.

DOORMAT FAITH

Befor the great disappearance of our dogs, I walked out my back door one day, and tripped over a hulking animal sprawled on the concrete. Jack, the black lab, didn't dare move as it might disturb his dreams of chasing rabbits or other such doggy pursuits. It was then that I accidentally dropped my keys on his head. The jingling and the jangling caused Jack to shake the dream off, but being an energy conservationist, movement was minimal. He did turn that massive head in my direction and look at me with those big brown eyes. Jack seemed to long for a hello, a pat on the head or an apology for rudely disturbing his rest. After rubbing my big ol' dog and telling him "I'm sorry if I ruffled your fur," I got to thinking of the dreaded analogy.

There that huge mutt was lying at the door, acting like a doormat. I say doormat because he sure couldn't be called a gatekeeper. Nope, this ol' fellow was real hospitable, he'd let anyone step over him and come on in! He was comfortable in his little niche of the world. From the moment Jack located our family, he ooched up into this prone position right next to the French doors. It was about the extent of his activity. Feeling safe, nourished and protected, he fell into a deep coma-like sleep only to awaken if someone stepped on him, or if the dinner bell rang. That doorstep is the same address for many of us Christians.

We take up residence at the doorstep of salvation, never pressing further than the entryway. Slumbering, our eyes only open and look in God's direction when our peace is disturbed, when we're hurt, when we're hungry or when we're scared.

I'm telling you this was a wake up call, no pun intended, for me. Remaining at the door of God's saving grace only to show signs of life when I have a problem is NOT where I want to be found. Being about my Master's business is much more satisfying. And honey, I'm here to tell you, staying at the place of entry can be dangerous! It's been said if you hang around right where you got in, you might be apt to fall back out.

Here's another rub! "Welcome" is written on the doormat of the entrance side and "Apathy" is penned on the other if we, like Jack, hunker down for a long life's nap. Jack's one mission in life is to rest in being safe. What a symbol of those of us who haven't pressed in farther in our relationship with Christ. We have become like that humongous Lab. We are stiff and unexercised. We are fat from being too comfortable and too complacent with God's wonderful gift of salvation. We need to get up and chase the frisbee. Let scripture be the key that knocks us out of our sleep. Let it be the final ruffling of the fur that puts the bite back in the bark. "WAKE UP, O SLEEPER, RISE FROM THE DEAD AND CHRIST WILL SHINE ON YOU." That's right! Stretch it out! Shake it off! YOU CAN DO IT!

❀ ❀ ❀ ❀ ❀ ❀ ❀

Breaking ground, y'all – – I am putting myself under the microscope of scripture and prayer. Will you join me?

When you examine your life by the light of the Word and ask God to reveal in you Himself, do you see movement, signs of life? My pastor is a retired thoracic surgeon; he understands pulse. He says when a person is rushed into the emergency room, the physicians don't check to see if the patient is dead; they check for signs of life. Are there signs evident in your life that you're spiritually alive? Are you pressing in? Are you bearing fruit? Join me as we rise up from the doorstep to follow Christ!

Blossoms from The Book – Philippians 3:12-14 Not that I have already obtained all this, or have already been made perfect, but I press on to take hold of that for which Christ Jesus took hold of me. Brothers, I do not consider myself yet to have taken hold of it. But one thing I do: Forgetting what is behind and straining toward what is ahead, I press on toward the goal to win the prize for which God has called me heavenward in Christ Jesus. *II Peter 3:17-18* Therefore, dear friends, since you already know this, be on your guard so that you may not be carried away by the error of lawless men and fall from your secure position. But grow in the grace and knowledge of our Lord and Savior Jesus Christ. To him be glory both now and forever, amen!

Petals of Petition – Oh, our Father in Heaven! How many times You have given me a wake-up call making me realize that I am living in the lap of complacency, happy for You just to have saved me. I know how easy it is, Father, to lose ground, to get fat and lazy when I stop studying Your word, or when I get too busy to pray and when I just go about MY business. Forgive me, Lord. Deep calls unto deep. Give me courage and strength to get out of the boat and walk with You! In Jesus' name, Amen.

CESSPOOLS OF HEALING

Sprawled on the floor, Mama, Daddy and three-year-old Lauren were just finishing their final game of Candyland. It was a night of making memories and chalking up wins, and little Lauren was the clear victor. The big people were tired and ready to turn out the lights, but Lauren, who was still feeling triumphant and a lot older than her three years, was anything but ready to sleep. Nope, this win had triggered something in her that made her want to share her status as the intelligent one. She smugly decided that she had within herself the makings of a doctor.

So as Mama picked up the pieces and went to put the game up for another day, Lauren looked at her Daddy with concern in her eyes. What she saw before her was a sucker for attention and a possible patient. Hence she said, "Dad, your eye looks sick. Lay down on the floor, and I will doctor you!"

After briefly leaving the room to obtain medical supplies, she scampered back to a tired and resting daddy who limply awaited her ministering hand. Lauren began to apply wet compresses (socks dipped in liquid) to the offensive eye. She expanded the area of attention to cover both of Dad's eyes, his nose and his mouth. The little nurse kept up a steady stream of words of healing as the medicinal water trickled down his cheeks into his ears and mouth. But another voice came through a little clearer and the words reaching his ears were anything but therapeutic. Mama was hollering from the hall, "Honey, that's toilet water! Don't use that on Daddy!"

With the agility of a young athlete, Daddy sprang from the floor, sputtering and spewing as his feet hit the ground.

Being no spring chicken, he was miraculously moved from lethargy to action in one swiftly uttered sentence.

You may ask how this has spiritual application, but there is always a bit of knowledge to be gleaned from every event. Have you ever been so tired that you didn't care what, why or how? Nothing mattered except that you were being ministered to and it didn't require any thought on your part? Maybe a little flattery was what you needed to hear, and the con artist won your ear. Did you just need to feel good, and you were so tired it didn't matter how that outcome was achieved? In Isaiah the 30th chapter, the rebellious Israelites were right there. They didn't want to be taught. They just wanted to "experience pleasant things." Deceptive things that would ultimately cause them to stray from the paths of truth, just as they tend to take us off the path God has set before us.

So, just as Dad, prostrate on the floor, accepted without question, the "medicinal waters," we too might be caught off-guard. We might quickly find that the attention that feels good just "ain't" the medicine we need. One final note – it's good to know that even though we do mess up and accept detrimental aid, we can spring from the cesspools when truth shouts its volumes. The truth will set you free!

Even three-year old Lauren got the message. In her words, truth is, "Dad doesn't like toilet water on his face. He will take his water from the sink." I'd just like to add, "Don't take it from the world, take it from the WORD."

❀ ❀ ❀ ❀ ❀ ❀ ❀ ❀

Breaking ground, y'all – I don't know about y'all, but there are days when I'm so tired, I just don't care about much. This is a dangerous state. Our guard is down and we are too tired to deal with double-checking with God on what is being said to us or done to us; we just accept it at face value. We do have a responsibility to test things to see how they line up with the Word of God. We really need to examine our motives, our plans and our actions. Do they fall out on the side of God's standards or with the world's standards? We will eventually end up in the sewer if we allow waste to seep into our lives!

Blossoms from The Book – Amos 6:4-7 You lie on beds inlaid with ivory and lounge on your couches. You dine on choice lambs and fattened calves. You strum away on your harps like David and improvise on musical instruments. You drink wine by the bowlful and use the finest lotions, but you do not grieve over the ruin of Joseph. Therefore you will be among the first to go into exile; your feasting and lounging will end. ***I Thessalonians 5:21-22*** Test everything. Hold on to the good. Avoid every kind of evil. ***Ephesians 5:14-15*** …for it is light that makes everything visible. This is why it is said: "Wake up, O sleeper, rise from the dead, and Christ will shine on you." Be very careful, then, how you live – not as unwise but as wise.

Petals of Petition – Father, please keep us vigilant, awake and on guard against the wiles of the enemy. Thank You that when we are weary, You will give us the strength and the stamina to carry on in the wisdom You share with us. Thank You for the gift of the Holy Spirit who teaches us, encourages us, and chastens us when we do get lazy and off-track. Oh Lord, help us to keep Your Word as the measuring stick by which we operate. Keep the world and the standards set there from blinding us from Your truth. Keep us out of the sewer. Praise You, Father. In Jesus' name, Amen.

5
WATERIN' SOIL

WHERE IS IT?

The following is written with the permission of my spouse and a dozen other friends who find themselves singing the same song.

Pick the melody, here's the chorus. Where oh where is my? Turn on the record. It's a new day and those words are playing in my head again! SHHHHH – listen. Many of you recognize the woeful crooning. I believe it's a "male call." Unlike a "mail call" that beckons us to receive something, this "male call" is hunting for something lost. AAAHH, there it goes again. It's a bewildered voice singing his morning song. Following the notes as they waft down the hall, I find my husband standing like a deer in headlights, in front of his dresser, a lost little boy look in his eye as he peers in a drawer. The record being played from vocal chords catches and begins to skip. It's stuck on "Kandi, Where's my?"

Yes, his actions are familiar. Without disturbing any of the contents, he continues this morning musical rendition of, "Where are my _____ ?" This isn't a name that tune quiz; I know you can hum the jingle, you can write your own verse. The socks, the shoes, the briefcase, the remote, the hairbrush are a few of my husband's choices that we can use to plug in the blank. The hairbrush is my personal favorite "Where is it?" It conjures up a real picture of humor. Here's the photograph. My husband who sports a military style haircut stands next to a vanity upon which five hairbrushes are ready for the choosing and he cries, "Honey, where's MY favorite brush?"

The morning litany continues as my sweet fellow heads for the door hollering, "Honey, where are my keys?" Once those babies are located, he finally makes it out the door, but I know it's not over till it's over. It's the same every day, just like clockwork, I can count one, two, three and he's back. "Honey, do you know where I put my wallet?"

Ah, the predictability of life! On a morning after an especially long list of "where's " I felt blessed to be at work. Upon entering the radio station and settling down to begin the day, the door of the studio opened. In walked my boss. "Kandi, do you know where?"

❀ ❀ ❀ ❀ ❀ ❀ ❀ ❀

Breaking ground, y'all – Lest you think that our house is a pigsty or disorganized to the hilt, let me say all this "where" stuff is habit. It's Lowry's theme song. My husband simply just depends on me to sing the answering verse. Now, I like it when my husband needs me, job security and all that, but it puts me in mind of how dependent we become on others. How often do we find ourselves relying on others for the really important things in life? I'm taking inventory myself, that self-examination thing. Maybe you'll join me under the tuning fork. Let's be positive that we are not relying on someone else for our faith. You know, believing just because we are the child or grandchild of a Godly man or woman, we can be grandfathered into the faith. We will stand alone before the Father. Others might point out the directions, but we have to do the finding. There are some things we just have to discover on our own. Anything less just doesn't ring true.

Blossoms from The Book – *II Chronicles 15:15b* …they sought God eagerly, and he was found by them. So the Lord gave them rest on every side. *I Corinthians 15:55-57* "Where, O death, is your victory? Where, O death, is your sting?" The sting of death is sin, and the power of sin is the law. But thanks be to God! He gives us the victory through our Lord Jesus Christ.

Petals of Petition – Father, many days we weary of looking for answers. God help us to come to You. Help us not to be dependent on others to get us out of jams or for others to change our circumstances. Please God, help us to seek You with all our heart, mind, soul and strength. Your Word is true. Thank you that the answer, the hope and the joy WILL be found in You. In Jesus' name, Amen.

A PURPOSE AND A PLAN

He came out of the woods, a skittish, but frightening canine. He appeared to be a dog that no one wanted or would want in the future. It was pretty apparent if you stood around long enough, you'd be able to see the fleas hopping from hair to hair. It's a good thing it wasn't my yard that this Chow-mix dog showed up in because I'm not sure the ol' dog bowl would have been filled with food. Dogs are pretty smart about things like that. These throw-away pooches seem to choose their masters. The mongrels that have been relocated to our neighborhood have proven that point by being selective about which doorstep they decide upon. The aforementioned dog chose my neighbors. Wise choice.

Susie, Guy and their daughter Shelby weren't too sure about this animal either. He was rough looking, y'all, and wild-eyed from abuse, but he seemed to realize that these folks would at the very least leave out some food. It took two months for any of them to even get within five feet of the pooch; he just showed up for chow. He was such a mangy, matted thing that he was aptly named "Rugrat." No one was quite sure how this animal was going to work out. Would he be a biter? Would he ever get over his fear? Was he redeemable? Little Shelby seemed to think he was worth keeping.

It took months of leaving a bowl of food out before ol' Rugrat even thought about trusting these humans, and then it was just a tentative move of allowing them to come a tad closer. It was like he had an invisible force field that was up at all times. Susie was determined to zap the barrier and get the dog to the vet for shots. It took a mammoth move to get him there, but she did it and with all her appendages remaining intact. The vet also survived, and Rugrat came back to the yard to exist. Now, the Clays always go a little farther than I do in the care of their animals. They make sure that even the outside dogs stay groomed and flea-free. This dog had indeed made the right choice, but it still wasn't obvious what place he had in their world. Even cleaned up he was a strange pup, and he could put the fear in this ol' gal.

For four years my neighbors questioned why Rugrat was still gracing them with his presence—that is until now. You see, this week Rugrat did an amazing thing. He saved Shelby's life. If you don't believe, just ask her mom and my husband. Susie and Shelby were driving in from school like they do every afternoon. They drove up to the partially opened garage where Rugrat stood barricading their entry. He was yappin' up a storm and he wasn't about to move. When Susie pushed the clicker to raise the garage door, she carefully scanned the garage from the safety of the car.

She saw a four- and-a-half foot rattle snake coiled and ready to strike lying right where Shelby would have stepped when getting out of the car. Rugrat raced in for the fight, protecting his family.

A lot of humans are like Rugrat. People look at them as the throwaways. They come into our world carrying their own brand of fleas, and just rubbing elbows with them makes you itch and ya' wonder. You can't imagine them ever coming clean. But once spic and span, there are always the doubters who say it won't last. I would have to agree it would be a tremendous feat if they returned to their original environment. It's like throwing a dipped dog back into an untreated pen. It won't be long before he's scratching again. But all deserve the chance to be helped even if we can't predict the outcome. There are those who enter our world and we wonder what purpose they have in it. God says that He would not have any perish...and he has given each of us a purpose!

❊ ❊ ❊ ❊ ❊ ❊ ❊ ❊

Breaking ground, y'all – I am ashamed to say it, but I have looked at people and thought, "How in the world can they be changed? They will never be any different than they are now. What could they do for the kingdom?" How arrogant and how small my faith. Have you given up on someone? Are there people in your circle of acquaintances that seem to be out of step with our understanding of useable? Oh, that God would give us eyes to see as He sees us!

Blossoms from The Book – I Samuel 16:7 But the LORD said to Samuel, "Do not consider his appearance or his height, for I have rejected him. The LORD does not look at the things man looks at. Man looks at the outward appearance, but the LORD looks at the heart." *I Corinthians 5:17* Therefore, if anyone is in Christ, he is a new creation; the old has gone, the new has come! *Jeremiah 29:11* For I know the plans I have for you," declares the LORD, plans to prosper you and not to harm you, plans to give you hope and a future. *Philippians 1:6* ...being confident of this, that he who began a good work in you will carry it on to completion until the day of Christ Jesus.

Petals of Petition –Father, I cry out for forgiveness, for I have looked upon what You have fearfully and wonderfully made and have questioned Your ability to mold a life that is surrendered to You. Help me to remember Lord, that You desire to take the foolish and confound the wise, that Your thoughts toward ALL of us are precious. You, Lord, the God of all Creation consider each of us to be people who can be transformed by the power of the Holy Spirit, if we will just walk by the Spirit. Oh, I thank you that there are NO throw-a-way people, but children of the King, sinners saved by grace! Thank you that we have purpose, to be passionate bearers of the Good News. Help us to see with Your eyes and to love with Your heart today. In Jesus' name, Amen.

MERCY ME!

Zing! Morning has broken and the battle has begun. It's an age-old war that usually rears its head with the first squeak of the closet door opening. Yep, that one little sound is a war cry in a home that houses siblings. It's time to put on your flak jacket as clothes begin to fly across the room like guided missiles and the verbal volleys break through the last vestige of peace in the home.

Do you recognize the morning battle cry of, "Where's my blouse? You better not have it because if you do and it's dirty, I'm coming after you!" Without pausing for breath, the barrage of accusatory words continues, "I can't believe you're in my stuff again. I can't ever find anything that belongs to me."

An echo of allegations is being launched from across the hall, "Well, I wouldn't have taken it if I could find any of my clothes. You wore my blouse last week and it's in the dirty clothes!"

Been there, done that war, weathered those skirmishes. With only one daughter at home, the dust has settled; not so with my friend, Debbie. Her girls were still breathing each other's air and they were in the throes of the clothing conflict daily. AAAAHHH, it was time to send for a professional, a mediator skilled in negotiating. The best was sent into the danger zone – her name? MOM.

With the skill of a pricey mediation team, a peace treaty was drawn up with retribution provisions for those who failed to comply with the terms. The penalties were severe. If one or the other sister was caught wearing the other's clothes, it would cost them where it hurts the most, their pocketbook, and the price was high.

Wouldn't you know, the younger sister, right off the bat, put on a shirt that belonged to her older sister? Sarah had had the blouse in her closet for so long that she'd forgotten that it wasn't hers! Upon seeing the look in her sister's eye, her memory returned. Having realized the error of her dress, she waited for the dreaded hammer to be dropped, the fireworks to fly and her purse to be lightened. To her surprise, big sis Christine, who just finished a morning devotion on mercy, granted clemency. Yep, she let her off the hook.

Mercy reigned.

Christine, now late to class because of this latest clash, put the pedal to the metal and sped on to school. To her dismay she was going to be a tad bit later. In her rearview mirror she caught the flash of blue lights and it sure wasn't the blue light special. This rotating flash of blue was accompanied by the breathtaking melody of sirens. Having pulled her over, the officer approached. She confessed that her foot had been heavy and she awaited her punishment, but alas, a warning was all that was forthcoming.

Whew, mercy! That's it, y'all..MERCY.

Do you notice scripture being fleshed out? Do you get the picture of grace? Blessed are the merciful, for they will be shown mercy. Got a war going on in your life? Feel like grenades are being launched? Want to fight? Fight with the most powerful weapon we have been afforded, merciful grace. It makes a beautiful outfit. Try it on for size. One size fits all, in a style called Grace, designed by God.

❀ ❀ ❀ ❀ ❀ ❀ ❀ ❀

Breaking ground, y'all – Okay, how many of your households resound with the fussing of siblings? How many of us pay back as good as we've gotten? Oh, when we do, what an angry mess remains! Sometimes, I forget just how much grace and mercy I have been given and I turn around and instead of extending the same to others, I goof and do just the opposite. It always amazes me, though, when I do follow God's principles and offer the mercy I have received, how much joy and peace fills the place.

Blossoms from The Book – Psalm 51:1-2 Have mercy on

me, O God, according to your unfailing love; according to your great compassion blot out my transgressions. *Zechariah 7:8-10* And the word of the LORD came again to Zechariah: This is what the LORD Almighty says: Administer true justice; show mercy and compassion to one another. Do not oppress the widow or the fatherless, the alien or the poor. In your hearts do not think evil of each other. *Matthew 5:7* Blessed are the merciful, for they will be shown mercy.

Petals of Petition – Father, how precious is Your mercy that is extended just for the asking. Help me to remember that Your grace is free, but oh, how expensive it was for You. When the situation arises for me to share forgiveness to someone, please remind me of that cost to You, and how You, knowing my sinful nature, loved me anyway. Remind me so that I might not be stingy, but freely giving in the same way. I love You Lord; help me walk in obedience to You even when I would like to get back at someone who has hurt me or someone I love. Thank you, again, Precious Savior for mercy. In Jesus' name, Amen.

ORANGE JULIUS

Moses, the beta fish, was a member of my daughter's family for four years. Now, this little fellow lived through some pretty traumatic times—a fishbowl stuffed with cornbread, a swim with Lauren in the tub, the list could go on and on. Moses must have longed for the opportunity to part the waters of his bowl and split the scene, but for four long years he managed to cope with his surroundings before going belly-up.

Speaking of coping and fish, let me tell you about this one! I've heard some strange names before, but a fish named

North? That was a new one on this ol' gal, but there was a motivation for the madness of this moniker. The fish, a member of the carp family, had been placed in a fairly large aquarium, but quickly grew to such humongous proportions that his body could only face one way, North. Lest anyone become disturbed about the environment of this fish, measures were taken to set North free. He was moving from a prison to a pond.

Cecil B. DeMille, (Steven Spielberg to you younger readers), would have been proud of the production made of the releasing of North. Colton, the fish's owner, his dad, my husband and I were all there to witness the big fish in the bowl become the little fish in the pond. We felt his joy at knowing forward movement, we could sense his delight at finding new delicacies to munch, and we shared his fear when a' detachment of bass bombers were deployed to investigate his liberation. In my husband's words, "As soon as Ol' North hit the clear waters of his new home, he was immediately trailed by what seemed to be a squadron of F-15 Fighter Jets. In reality, they were the hungry advances of large mouth bass.

We grown-ups were filled with panic as we watched this disturbing appearance of hungry warlords. We just knew Colton's eyes were going to require shielding from the banquet that was about to take place. But to our surprise, North managed to work a game plan. Having tested the deeper waters and finding them completely unsafe, he honed in on the grassy shallows – and there he set up housekeeping. The bigger fish tired of waiting for North to venture into enemy territory. They left the little guy alone and he seemed to understand that it was vitally important to his health for him to remain inside a certain perimeter, the boundaries that secured his safety. Nowadays when Colton and his sister Kayla come for visitation, we go outside to the pond. North is immediately visible, as he has gone from a pasty pale white to a brilliant orange. He now bears a better name; he's known to all as Orange Julius. The old has gone and the new has come.

Yep, ol' Moses, my granddaughter's fish, had managed to live a fairly decent life for a long time in a pretty precarious environment. He will be missed. North, on the other hand had outgrown his and was set free to live in a dangerous environment. But he learned that margins were necessary for his survival. Many of us have families that are growing up on us. There comes a time when they are outgrowing us and needing to. Ooooh, that's hard to admit, our little fish outgrowing the protective waters of home. Keeping them constantly in familiar waters, never letting them test new waters, to expand their territory, to trust them, is to stunt their growth. Release them to grow!

❀ ❀ ❀ ❀ ❀ ❀ ❀ ❀

Breaking ground, y'all – Every day it's graduation time for some. Our children are growing up and many of them are leaving the nest. I've been up close and personal on this one. I've watched as young people are expanding their territories, becoming little fish in big ponds. Let's you and I join in a common prayer for them to have the wisdom to realize that there are a lot of temptations lining up to eat their lunch, the understanding to know that remaining in the borders of their faith will keep them safe and that they will grow to be the attractive adults God called them to be.

Blossoms from The Book – Proverbs 3:1-2 Do not forget my teaching, but keep my commands in your heart, for they will prolong your life many years and bring you prosperity. *Galatians 5:1* It is for freedom that Christ has set us free. Stand firm, then, and do not let yourselves be burdened again by a yoke of slavery.

Petals of Petition – Father, oh, we are so grateful that You have allowed us the privilege of caring for Your precious gifts, the treasure of children, and of those You have given us to disciple. Gently lead us in the training and daily leadership of our charges, but help us to remember to hold loosely to these gifts. Please give us the courage to let them go when You say it's time. When the time comes to send them out, keep them in Your hands and guide them. As they venture into the world, please remind them of the safety of boundaries, the wisdom to use what they have been taught, and most of all, Father, to stay close to You. Lead them not into temptation, but deliver them from evil. We love You, Lord and trust You! In Jesus' name, Amen.

LOSING GROUND

Since you're taking the time to read this book, I figure we're getting to be fairly good buddies, and good buddies tend to share secret stories. So, shhhhh! Put a finger to your lips and flip those sunglasses over your eyes as you read the following. Let this be between you and me and please, try to keep it under your hat. This ol' tale just might embarrass and humiliate someone near and dear to me!

We live on acreage on the outskirts of town. It's a bit of a stretch just keeping the place mowed. Summer was upon us and we were faced with one of those household dilemmas— we were without a riding mower. We made it a matter of prayer. Sure we could have push-mowed through the land mass. It had been done on several occasions, but we

were getting older. Plus, time was a precious commodity
and so were our arthritic limbs. We didn't know what we
were going to do, short of floating a loan. God did. I just
love the creativity of the Father. A precious young girl in
our Sunday school class also had a need. Jennifer had one
of those snazzy, shore 'nuff lawn mowers and no place to
keep it out of the weather. Since the Anderson family had
storage space, a lot of yardage to cut and no lawn mower,
we struck an awesome trade: we store, we use. You might
be questioning why someone with several acres would be
minus a riding lawnmower in the first place. Well, that's
the thing we didn't want leaking out to just anyone. It's
pretty embarrassing. We sunk the thing. I say "we" simply
because "the two shall be one," and that's about all the responsibility I'm taking!

In the prior year a bad dry spell had paid us a visit.
Some called it "the big drought." The water levels sank so
low that the ponds began to shrink. Weedy grass that hadn't
seen the light of day in a long time began to shoot up and
I'm here to tell you that whet my husband's appetite. His
love for mowing is a well-known fact among the neighborhood and when he spied that newly-exposed grass
around the pond's edge, his eyes took on a weird gleam.
He revved his engine and prepared to nip those sprouts in
the bud. He put the mower in gear and zoomed out to the
reservoir of water. With the tenacity of a goat spying fresh
greens, he had the blades of that mower snipping at the
grass closest to the water when suddenly the rear tire began to slide and glide. Jumping off the lawn mower, he tried
to get a toehold and grab the mower. It just wasn't
happening. My muscle bound man couldn't get a lock on
that plummeting hulk of metal and every shred of resis-
tance dissolved as the mower slid down into the murky

waters. He said the last thing he remembered was the hiss of hot metal hitting water followed by an awful gurgling, sinking sound. SSSSsssss, blub blub blub. Once pulled out, it fizzled out. So, be careful my friends if you are flirting with life's slippery slopes – don't. It's too easy to fall in and sizzle.

Oh, yeah, just for the record, remember, let's keep this story between ourselves – my husband's ego couldn't stand another dunking.

❀ ❀ ❀ ❀ ❀ ❀ ❀

Breaking ground, y'all – This little slip into the pond left me soaking in some spiritual applications. One, when our lives get dry and we aren't prayed up and fellowshipping with believers, the weeds in our life start to grow and are exposed. The drought leaves us spiritually dehydrated and we tend to look for any way to quench our thirst. We scoot closer to the edge of sin trying to fill our lives with anything wet. The closer we get to the edge, the easier it is to slide into the abyss, and experience has it— if you don't dry off quickly, you can end up like our lawnmower— rusted out and useless.

Blossoms from The Book – *Psalm 73:2-3* But as for me, my feet had almost slipped; I had nearly lost my foothold. For I envied the arrogant when I saw the prosperity of the wicked. *Psalm 73:16-19* When I tried to understand all this, it was oppressive to me 'til I entered the sanctuary of God; then I understood their final destiny. Surely you place them on slippery ground; you cast them down to ruin. How suddenly are they destroyed, completely swept away by terrors! *Psalm 94:17-19* Unless the LORD had given me help,

I would soon have dwelt in the silence of death. When I said, "My foot is slipping," your love, O LORD, supported me. When anxiety was great within me, your consolation brought joy to my soul.

Petals of Petition – Oh Father, there have been far too many times in my life when I was in a dry land and sought for relief in the wrong places, getting closer and closer to the slippery edges of captivity. Forgive me. Restore me. Keep my feet from slipping. Father, help me and those who join me in this battle to steady ourselves in You, to be filled and spilling over with the power, grace and mercy found in You. I don't want to rust out, or burn out by the corrupting forces of evil, but I want to be spent and used by You. Thank you, Lord, that You rescue and make level our paths and satisfy our thirst! In Jesus' name, Amen.

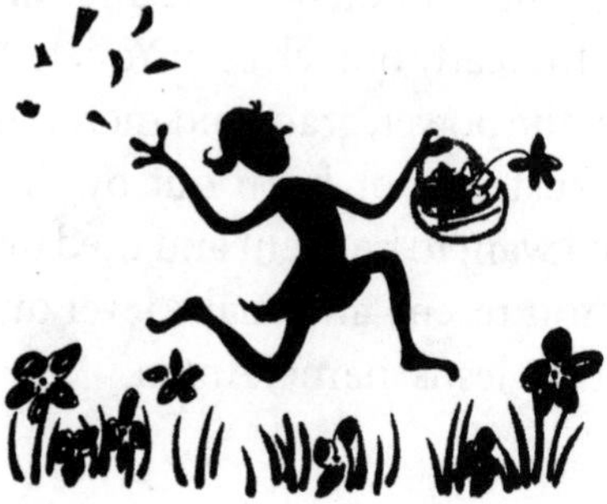

6

PULLIN' WEEDS

MISS THE SIGNS?

Miss the signs? It was clear that I wasn't missing the signs of a problem when a shrill, shaky voice said, "Mom, I need to tell you something." My muscles cringe at the sound of that line, don't yours? I braced myself as a rapid-fire description of the dilemma unfolded. Apparently, my youngest daughter had missed a sign – one indicating the speed limit – and she had a little blue piece of paper to show for her oversight. Her explanation of said ticket was worthy of print.

Yes, I raised blonde children, intelligent blonde children. There are lapses though, little skips, at times major jumps in their cognitive thinking. My child's tale of trouble went like this: "Mom, I had just left the church on the beach when I was driving up Highway 49 and I SAW the policeman behind me. He followed me for several blocks and I know how it must really bother them when traffic slows down when they show up, so I went 5 miles over the speed limit. I thought I was doing him a favor!" I thought, "Right, five miles per hour faster, you know, that mythical leeway on the speedometer."

Kasie said it just shocked the fire out of her when she saw the blue lights flash, signaling her to stop. I can see the wheels in her mind turning to the tune of, "Me? You are pulling ME over?" When the policeman proceeded to ask her the question he already knew the answer to, "Do you know how fast you were going?" My daughter, assuming she was innocent as a lamb, answered, "Yes sir, I was going five miles over." Now, here's the clincher, the ticket winning final addition to that statement. She had the audacity to add, "Sir, I thought I was doing you a favor. I know how you must hate it when people go the speed limit." Now, that line alone was worth a chunk of change.

I thought, "Wow, that's what it costs when you go five miles over the speed limit?" May I inform you I now know that she didn't exceed the limit by a mere five miles an hour. Nope it was a tad more. Apparently not everyone is aware that the speed limit differs near the beach! It's a whole lot slower. It's been my favorite quiz question of late, asking people in the know if they knew. Most did not. You travel a road for years; you think you know every nuance of the thing. "Thought" is the key word. Sometimes, it's necessary for people who think they're right to check it out just to prove a point. So skeptic that I am, I checked. There were four, count them, four speed limit signs indicating 35 miles per hour. Gotcha. Got me. Got her. We all missed the signs!

❀ ❀ ❀ ❀ ❀ ❀ ❀ ❀

Breaking ground, y'all –Deceived and ticketed. Ouch, that costs. When we take for granted that we've got it right just because "it's always been done that way," or "I thought," we stand to lose. The proverbial "Everybody else does it," just doesn't mean much in the light of truth. As you're merrily tooling down life's road, trying to please everyone, attempting to feel good and maybe, just maybe, step a little over the line of the correct, pull over and check the signs to be sure you know that you know. I John 5:11-12 is a billboard of Truth for me. And this is the testimony: God has given us eternal life, and this life is in his Son. He who has the Son has life; he who does not have the Son does not have life. It's personal and the ticket at the end has either been paid or it's going to cost too much. Miss the signs?

Blossoms from The Book – Colossions 3:8 See to it that no one takes you captive through hollow and deceptive philosophy, which depends on human tradition and the basic principles of this world rather than on Christ. ***Psalm 19:1-2*** The heavens declare the glory of God; the skies proclaim the work of his hands. Day after day they pour forth speech; night after night they display knowledge. ***Psalm 92: 5-6*** How great are your works, O LORD, how profound your thoughts! The senseless man does not know, fools do not understand….

Petals of Petition – Father, Help us to be vigilant, to stay in the Word, to seek Your ways. Oh Lord, keep our hearts from deception. Open our eyes to the signs. Help us to proclaim to others the Truth of Your Word, the glorious joy of being Your children! Lord, time is short and the danger too great if we do not remain on constant guard. May we be found diligent, and studying so that we might show ourselves approved and be able to give a reason for the hope that is within us. Thank You that we are never left in the dark, for You are the Light! In Jesus' name, Amen.

CLEANIN' UP THE ACT

Opening the door to find a large speckled trout head glaring up at me with a dead stare is not, let me repeat that, not the way I like to begin my day. We thought the ol' boy had cleaned up his act. We actually believed he was on the road to recovery. Of whom do I speak? That would be Clark, a canine gift, a disaster waiting to happen. He leaves a wake of destruction in his path that would make a pig blush. Yes, Clark can break through to the core of a golf ball in short order, leaving the insides stringing across the porch – and that's just one of his tricks. He has a thing about people watching TV. In short order he can spy a neatly hidden cable line, pull it plumb off an outside brick wall and then mangle it until there is no possibility of airwaves ever traveling through it again. He has a real problem with being outside when the action is happening inside.

He yearns to be a part of the group, and when the intensity of his longing peaks, he'll take a running leap at a window hoping to gain entry, cracking the glass on impact. He enjoys pillaging the woods and bringing his plunder home for inspection. It doesn't stop there. Oh, no. Some eat for nourishment, Clark chews on everything just because he can. He cannot stand clean. Clark is our bad dog, and the delivery boy of dead fish.

With company coming, and the landscape of our yard looking like we had a ground hog on the loose as well as a demolition crew that forgot to clean up after the explosion, my husband Lowry spent a couple of hours picking up, throwing away, bleaching, window washing, and restoring cable. Clark looked a tad bewildered, but content with his new surroundings. It seemed that he was actually pleased with clean living. In fact, Lowry confirmed that thought by informing us, "Clark is reformed. I believe we have lived through puppyhood." That is, until I opened the door and just about planted my foot on the speckled trout head. With a shrill, loud voice I announced that Clark had fallen off the wagon and his fondness for the filthy had returned with a smelly vengeance. Trying to rid my mind's eye of scales and smells, I began to ponder the lesson that might be in the middle of this mess.

Had we enabled Clark? Were we co-dependent? Did we clean up after him, not teaching him good things to occupy the blank spots in his days? Were we so busy with our lives that the ol' boy wasn't receiving the attention he craved? Oh, many are the trials of life, and it's a little scary that a fish head can cause my mind to "think on these things." The theology may be a little shallow, but ponder it a bit. Fill 'er up with the good stuff. Take time with those you love and teach 'em well. I've got to go now; Obedience School, anyone?

❀ ❀ ❀ ❀ ❀ ❀ ❀ ❀

Breaking ground, y'all – So many times I have tried to clean up for others. I have stepped in and tried to right a wrong or pull someone out of the fire, all with good intentions and hopeful motives. For a season it seemed to help, but often the dilemma, the demon itself returned with ugly vigor. Could it be that because I did the bailing, that poor sinking soul didn't have to lift a finger and later assumed it was rescue time again? Each clean-up swept the old junk away, but nothing good replaced the bad habits. It was easier to just do it myself than to teach, train, pray and then let go and let them.

Blossoms from The Book – Matthew 12:43-35 When an evil spirit comes out of a man, it goes through arid places seeking rest and does not find it. Then it says, 'I will return to the house I left.' When it arrives, it finds the house unoccupied, swept clean and put in order. Then it goes and takes with it seven other spirits more wicked than itself, and they go in and live there. And the final condition of that man is worse than the first. *John 5:14* Afterward Jesus found him in the temple, and said to him, "See, you have been made well. Sin no more, lest a worse thing come upon you."

Petals of Petition – Our Father, how often I try to take matters in my own hands, thinking I am up to fixing everybody's lives for them. Forgive me. I make such a mess when I run ahead of You and forget that You might be doing a work in someone, and that I might be interfering with Your plans. Help me to remember to trust You, Lord. Help me to remember that You are able. Father, please fill each of us with Your Holy Spirit, with Your Word and with the strength and wisdom to walk in obedience to you. Leave no empty spots for sin to fill. Lord, as we individually come before you and ask to be set free from the sin that so easily besets us, clean us up and fill us with the works that You would give us to do! Lead us not into temptation, but deliver us from sin and be glorified in us. In Jesus' name. Amen.

SOUP'S ON!

Ah, when there's a nip in the air, there's a spot in my tummy calling out for good ol' homemade soup. I believe everything that's ever been written about the medicinal qualities of soup. There's just something homey and feel-good about that delicious liquid. It doesn't matter what the flavor: chicken, vegetable, hearty potato, or creamy broccoli and cheese; it's all good. What does count is that it's homemade. Nothing less will satisfy.

So, when I get a hankering for a cup of broth, it's time to pull out that great big lugger of a pot and fill it up with a meaty soup bone, seasonings, onions, and water. I turn the heat up and cook it down. That's when something ugly begins to happen. Just about the time things begin to roll and boil, this "stuff" comes to the surface. It's kind of scummy looking and I have to skim it off the top before any of the finicky eaters come taking a peek at the pot.

What is this foamy mess? Who knows? I took a survey and was told that I needed to clean my veggies better. Another friend gave me some technical definition of the phenomenon. Whatever! I just keep dipping it out and the end result is a hearty broth to which I add those final scrumptious touches. UHMMM MMMM GOOD ... that's what a bowl of hot, homemade soup is to a chilled and hungry soul.

I was pondering life one day over a bowl of this delectable liquid when it hit me. My life, as of late, can be compared with cooking soup. My husband and I are branching out into new territory. Lowry, my compadre in life, was in the wholesale lumber business for 27 years. The key word here is "was." God moved us. He directed our paths and stretched our tents right into full-time ministry. Let me tell you, it gets a little chilly when you leave the warm nest of the familiar, but it doesn't take long for things to heat up.

When the temperature of life just keeps on rising, this scummy stuff just starts making its way to the top. It's not pretty. Have you been there? You start thinking and projecting. Now, pondering and over-analyzing can send the ol' thermometer soaring. Maybe your temperature burns at the thought of finances, your calendar, or the unknown. Well, can I share what God is teaching me? It wouldn't be appropriate for me to say what God has taught me because I'm still being simmered and seasoned. What I do know is that when the junk – fear, anger, weariness, crankiness and all the other junk boils up – I just ask God to skim it off. He cleans me up and stirs up the good stuff He has planted in my life. Just like a good pot of soup takes all day for the seasonings to blend in just right, it takes a lifetime of heating up, skimming off and flavoring for a life to be pleasing to the palate and to the Lord.

So next time you ladle up a savory bowl of soup, remember what it took to get it tasting mouth-watering good. Cup your hand and pull some of that fragrant aroma into your system and know steam is released from a well-cooked broth! And how awesome is the warmth that flows from the bowl of life skimmed and seasoned by the Savior!

❊ ❊ ❊ ❊ ❊ ❊ ❊ ❊

Breaking ground, y'all –In the pressure cooker of life, are you finding yourself in a full-blown boil, a slow simmer, or in a nice rolling heat? Have you asked God to show you what needs to come to the surface so it can't be removed? Sometimes it's not a pretty sight when God begins to reveal the junk that needs to be discarded, but keep your eye on the Cook. He knows what will make your life pleasing to Him and to others. Hang in there; a good cook is constantly on guard against sticking and burning, and we are in the hands of the best.

Blossoms from The Book – Titus 2:11-14 For the grace of God that brings salvation has appeared to all men. It teaches us to say "No" to ungodliness and worldly passions, and to live self-controlled, upright and godly lives in this present age, while we wait for the blessed hope – the glorious appearing of our great God and Savior, Jesus Christ, who gave himself for us to redeem us from all wickedness and to purify for Himself a people that are His very own, eager to do what is good.

Petals of Petition – Oh, heavenly Father, thank you that You are watching over us when the heat of plain ol' living begins to rise. We are so grateful that your heart is turned toward us despite the "stuff" that surfaces, that you are gentle to remove our imperfections and to forgive us of the sin. Please continue to get rid of the sin from our lives so that it won't spoil our witness or our fellowship with You. Thank you for your patient love and the touch of the Master's hand. In Jesus' name, Amen.

WRINKLES AND ALL

I was checking over my e-mail when I noticed a clearly common theme running through some personal notes from people I had visited during the week. All seemed to say, "thank you for being transparent." So much for the old-fashioned thoughts of being a woman of mystery and mystique! I am anything but. Oh, in some people's minds this attempt to be see-through might be considered dense. But maybe, just maybe, my ineptitude and lapses in perfection will help someone laugh and feel better that it's me and not them! So, I guess I'll share another leaf out of my life.

My pages are kind of wrinkled now as I have entered the years of grandparenthood. I've been looking for a painless eraser to remove a few of the creases of life. The answer showed up in the form of my youngest daughter's career pursuit. Kasie has decided to follow up on one of the talents that God's shared with her, the knack of making others feel better by improving on what they have been given. She's currently attending Chris' Beauty College, and the stuff she's studying is being applied to good ol' mom. That's right, just call me the human guinea pig, a live test case, the breathing mannequin. My hairstyle has never been so varied and interesting, but hair isn't all she's used as training ground. Nope, the scope is wider and the experimentation broader. Yes, I've even been the recent recipient of a peel. You read that correctly, the acid test.

Remember, my aforementioned, um, fine lines? Well, I got the phone call from the beauty school that they were offering a wrinkle reducer, the glycolic acid peel, and would I like to come down and be the beneficiary of this relaxing facial? There wasn't a hesitant laugh line in me. I showed up at the school thinking I was going to have a private session in the facial room, but that wasn't the case. Once again, my life was an open book, this time a living workbook. The class gathered around me as my face was unmasked, makeup removed, and every flaw exposed for the entire group. The product was properly applied and the peeling began. I'm sure to be on the next segment of SURVIVOR.

Looking back, I felt kind of funny, plopped in the chair, cape in place, hair pulled back, face starkly clean and stripped of dead skin. When my lids lifted, inquisitive eyeballs were peering down at my face, checking for results. It was then I had a spiritual moment. I realized that many times God allows our lives to be held up to the light of examination for all to see with the imperfections showing, His perfecting grace is not without effect!

Ah, the mystery of faith is revealed in letting His light shine on us and through us. I figure if you're going to be an open book, make sure the Author is making it a good read!

❀ ❀ ❀ ❀ ❀ ❀ ❀ ❀

Breaking ground, y'all –How often do we hide behind masks, unwilling to reveal the authenticity of who we are? We are all sinners, y'all. We all have need of the Savior. When His light shines on us, we are unmasked. When we ask Him to live in us, that Light shines through us. It's not always comfortable as layer-by-layer is stripped away, but scripture talks about shedding the old and putting off the new, and that my friend, is a good thing. Happy unveiling!

Blossoms from The Book – II Corinthians 3:16-18 But whenever anyone turns to the Lord, the veil is taken away. Now the Lord is the Spirit, and where the Spirit of the Lord is, there is freedom. And we, who with unveiled faces all reflect the Lord's glory, are being transformed into His likeness with ever-increasing glory, which comes from the Lord, who is the Spirit . *Philippians 2:15-16a* So that you may become blameless and pure, children of God without fault in a crooked and depraved generation, in which you shine like stars in the universe as you hold out the Word of Life.

Petals of Petition –Father in Heaven, reveal Yourself to us. Shine Your light on us, examine us and see if there be any wicked way in us. Cleanse us. Renew us. Help us to rid ourselves of the sins that would beset us. Help our lives to be transparent and shine through that others might see You in us and You be lifted up! In Jesus' name, Amen.

TRAPPED!

"People are so nice!" These were unusual words from a woman who had just experienced a terribly trying afternoon, but that's my mom for you. She was describing the chivalrous knights who had earlier rescued her from the terrors of modern technology. Supposedly the alarm system on her car had been disabled—mostly because it alarmed mom when it would inadvertently go off. When you least expected it, the thing would blast off, kind of like the Emergency Broadcast Announcement, BLEEEEEEP.

THIS IS A TEST. Apparently someone forgot to tell the alarm system that it had been rendered inoperable, because on several occasions it would decide to activate itself and scare the beejeebers out of her. Flustered, not knowing how to turn the sucker off, she would start to panic. But on this day these nice fellows came to her aid and shut the blaring down. Thanks guys!

As she shared this with me, I remembered an up-close and personal experience I recently had with an alarm system. No joyful noises to relate, just the facts. Sunday found my husband needing to be at church a couple hours before service and I tagged along for the ride. My intentions were to hibernate in my car while Lowry went inside. Ah, what a plan that was! Alone with a couple hours by myself with no dirty dishes, laundry or phone calling my name, I just knew it was going to be heaven. We pulled into the parking lot and Lowry hopped out of the car, locking the doors and leaving me to my book, a pleasant afternoon and an open sunroof. Thanks Lowry!

With the seat reclined back as far as she would go, I felt a bit like Mrs. Astor; but honey, not for long. Little did I know that shortly I'd be facing an emotionally debilitating episode. After a while I began to hear murmurings outside the car. Someone was saying, "I thought Lowry said Kandi was outside. I wonder where she could be?"

Now, I like a good game of hide-and-go-seek, but I knew I'd better speak up and let my friends know where I was holed up. I popped my head up just about the time they put their hands near the car door. BEEEEP. BEEEP. BEEEP. You got it. The car alarm was in full distress. I attempted to unbolt the car door, but the lock snapped shut as quickly as I tried to exit. This went on for longer than I care to think about. I was certain I was in a Stephen King movie. I wasn't claustrophobic before that night, but trauma will reduce you to new lows. Finally, we gave up the fight and located the man with the keys and I was rescued from the place I had wanted to be in the first place. Thanks keys.

Does that make any sense? I mean I wanted to be in that car, but when I was trapped, I sure was ready for the great escape. I was absolutely all set to tear my way out, shattering glass if need be, anything to get out of my prison. The key to being extricated from entrapment of sin is to recognize you're stuck in the middle of it and you want to get out and stay out. You might wrestle and think you can will yourself out, crash your way out, or extract yourself, but it's much simpler to say, "Lord, I don't want to be here. Forgive me. Help me. Deliver me." Thank you, Lord!

❀ ❀ ❀ ❀ ❀ ❀ ❀

Breaking ground, y'all – Isn't it funny that the very places we work hard to get into become places that trap us? Sin does that, too, doesn't it? It's attractive and beckons us and we can't wait to jump on the bus. But baby, once we find we can't get off, we struggle like crazy to flee, usually to no avail. It's like the door won't open on its own. Someone has to bring the keys.

Blossoms from The Book – Isaiah 33:6 He will be the sure foundation for your times, a rich store of salvation and wisdom and knowledge; the fear of the Lord is the key to this treasure! *John 8:34-36* Jesus replied, "I tell you the truth, everyone who sins is a slave to sin. Now a slave has no permanent place in the family, but a son belongs to it forever.

So if the Son sets you free, you will be free indeed!"

Petals of Petition – Father, how often I think I know what I want. Lord God, how often I have desired the things that are better left in Egypt. Forgive me, You have the best for me. You have set me free from the past by the blood of the Lamb. Thank you for opening the door to the sin that wanted to hold me captive, and thank You for giving me the strength through the power of Your Holy Spirit to keep from returning. We praise You Lord, for where You are there is freedom! In Jesus' name, Amen.

7
BLOOMIN' MIRACLES

THROUGH THE FIRE

Babies, Babies, Babies. I just love those cuddly bundles of love! Lowry and I have decided that one of the greatest joys in life is to be known as the grandparents of many women! The line-up as of this writing: our effusive six-year-old Lauren Brett; our California girl, 21-month-old Karlie Mae; our fearless 18-month-old Sadie Morgan; and our quietly changing two-month-old Madison Key. You would think my cup full! Honey, it is overflowing!

I still love to claim some babies that don't have the smell of baby powder and haven't for years; they are the guys and gals in our Sunday School Class. "Mixed Nuts" is a good moniker for such a diverse group of people, but in my mind, they are all my "babies." They are my joy and a prayer in my heart.

With so many to love, there tend to be those phone calls you get in the middle of the night or early in the morning that set your heart in rapid-fire mode and your teeth on edge. You almost don't want to answer, but know you must. The call came just at dawn and the message was about one of those strong, capable young'uns, one of those that we pray angels around because of the danger of his job. His name is Matt Nault and he is a firefighter.

Let me set the stage. Stacey, his wife had been getting

the two of them ready to head out on vacation. That's a mouthful right there! I'd like to be a fly on the wall watching these two packing anything. They are absolute perfectionists. I just toss and go, but they are sticklers for coordinating, and that's time consuming. Stacey was on the phone asking Matt to put the trip off for a day. He didn't want to, and the sparks flew. For the first and last time Stacey and Matt got off the phone mad as hornets.

Scene two. It's 3:20 a.m. and Stacey gets the call that Matt's been burned. The story continues. My husband and I always thought that in the middle of a fire you could see pretty clearly. In the movie's version of fire fighting you can distinctly visualize everything, so we just reasoned that the blaze would illuminate the scene. Not so. Matt said smoke engulfs a room resulting in little to zero visibility. In a pitch-black room, smoke billowing and rows and rows of merchandise and falling debris blocking aisles, it's impossible to find your way without having routines and patterns to follow. Even then you can become disoriented when your skin is burning, when you know you're the one that's smoldering.

Matt was burning and all his resources of finding his way out seemed to have collapsed around him. He lay down to die, to quit hurting. Through the fog of the smoky inferno and his excruciating pain, there came a loud hum. It was the familiar sound of the blowers used to push the smoke through the building. Something stood Matt up and he ran toward the noise, never tripping over a single piece of the debris surrounding him. Something pitched him headlong through the one plate glass window that didn't have bars, a window he didn't even know existed. But God knew, and God was that "something," that Someone, that led Matt from death to life.

Matt has had a long journey struggling to heal, but he is alive and this ol' mama hen is so thankful. I'd fight a buzz saw for Matt and those like him in our class; but I am inadequate. God isn't. He takes care of His children in the midst of the hottest of fires and the darkness of the night. And what He's done for others, He will do for you!

❀ ❀ ❀ ❀ ❀ ❀ ❀ ❀

Breaking ground, y'all – Matt couldn't see. He was in an unfamiliar place, but the voice of God came for Matt in the sound of a loud fan. The hand of God moved him past the stumbling blocks and the grace of God delivered him from the flames. That same God knows where you are today. If your world is dark, if you can't find your way and the pain is too great – remember this same God is your Deliverer and your Hope. Don't give up. Listen and run to the sound of His voice. He will never leave you or forsake you! A Postscript: Stacey would have you know that whatever you do, don't hang up mad, for every call is a chance to say I love you.

Blossoms from The Book – Psalm 143: 8-10 Let the morning bring me word of Your unfailing love, for I have put my trust in You. Show me the way I should go, for to You I lift up my soul. Rescue me from my enemies, O Lord, for I hide myself in You. Teach me to do Your will, for You are my God; may Your good spirit lead me on level ground. *Isaiah 43:1-2* But now, this is what the LORD says – He who created you, O Jacob, He who formed you, O Israel: "Fear not, for I have redeemed you; I have summoned you by name; you are Mine. When you pass through the waters, I will be with you; and when you pass through the rivers, they will not sweep over you. When you walk through the fire, you will not be burned; the flames will not set you ablaze.

Petals of Petition – Oh Father, how we come to You, thankful that nothing ever "dawns on You" and that You are keenly aware of all our dark nights. You call us and walk us through the flames of difficulty. Thank you for being the God of second chances, that we can learn from our mistakes and that we can see the need to follow Your Word, as we are not to let the sun go down on our anger. There is so much that we will never see this side of Glory, how You protect, heal and save. Through the trials You are constantly healing and teaching us. We praise You and thank you. In Jesus' name, Amen.

BUFFALO BLOCKADE

Hurry, hurry, hurry. Scurry, scurry, scurry. It seems that every day finds us stressed to the max. I used to think some months were worse than others, but not anymore. Every week demands so much of us, and our moods are reflected in the dispositions of our children, spouses, co-workers and anybody else who happens to get in our way! We are people in a hurry to have fun, in a rush to get the kids grown or just making ourselves crazy to make it to the dance lessons, karate lessons, and soccer practice on time!

Then there is absolutely no delaying our desire to furnish the house or to buy the boat. A little thing like having the money set aside is just too tough, takes too much discipline and besides, those guys who send us applications in the mail have the cash set aside for us to enjoy, now! And what about cooking a meal these days? I can't tell you when I had time or made the time to cook a full course meal.

Quick and easy, shake and bake is too long for this ol' gal. What about your children? Have you ever told them to wait? Wow, it's a lost art, an extinct practice, and a vocabulary word foreign to most.

I always find that when I have trouble with something, God supplies everything I need to learn – and sometimes it's painful. Pull up a chair, class is in session. A dear friend shared one of the most poignant examples of learning to wait and to trust; maybe we can gain some wisdom from her ordeal.

I can still remember where I was when I got the news that Shirley's son, 11 years old at the time, was fighting for his life. The walls of the church office seemed to shrink around us as we were told that little Allen Blacklidge, vacationing in Yellowstone Park with his family, had been struck by a Winnebago as he crossed a road. An immediate moaning of fervent prayer went heavenward for God to spare Allen. He did, but not without a pause.

Fourteen years later I asked Shirley about that day and the trip to the hospital. I can't even begin to imagine the horror of being in the middle of a gigantic forest watching the life breath ooze from your child. My stomach churns as I think what it must have been like to wait for helicopters to air evac your baby, not once, but twice. And the misery of not being able to accompany your child as he's whisked to a hospital in another state is incomprehensible. The last words Shirley remembers the medic saying as he put her child on board were, "I can't tell you anything."

With those words echoing in their ears, Randy and Shirley rushed to their car to make the three- and-a-half hour journey to their son's side—not knowing what they would find when they arrived. As they began their trek out of Yellowstone, the unexpected happened. A large herd of buffalo chose that moment to stroll across the road. There was no way to go around them, through them or to hasten them along. Shirley wanted to scream! Her vocal cords ached to scream for them to move, to shout for the rangers, something. All she could do was pray and trust God. Only the peace of God could stay the hand of insanity at such a dilemma. Only the Holy Spirit could show a frantic mom and dad that this was a picture of faith drawn just for them and they must endure the waiting. They did. Shirley said that was the moment God gently reminded them that they weren't in control. They certainly couldn't physically move those buffalo and they couldn't do anything about Allen. They would have to trust his life to his Father, their Father...God. They did and God was faithful. Allen stands a living miracle today.

Class is in session! Watch out, BUFFALO AHEAD!

❀ ❀ ❀ ❀ ❀ ❀ ❀ ❀

Breaking ground, y'all – The question is...Are you uncomfortable with the word "wait"? Are you ready to settle for an Ishmael? Sarah wanted to rush God's promise of a son. He wasn't acting quickly enough to suit her; therefore, she took matters into her own hands, making it happen. Not good. Do you feel like there are buffalo looming in your life? Are those big bison blocking your view of the future? Have those immense beasts meandered across the road you meant to travel? If they have, the answer is simple...wait. Then thank God, but don't you dare compromise your faith. I truly believe that the Word clearly shows that, "To compromise our faith, is as seen in this acrostic...to Cut Out My Promise," those promises of the Lord. We can trust the Father, even when we can't see the way.

Blossoms from The Book – Isaiah 42:16 I will lead the blind by ways they have not known, along unfamiliar paths I will guide them; I will turn the darkness into light before them and make the rough places smooth. These are the things I will do; I will not forsake them. *Psalm 40:1* I waited patiently for the Lord; He turned to me and heard my cry.

Petals of Petition – Father, oh how we need You as we face the giants in our lives! Thank you for the gentle, but clear reminders that we are not in control. You are. You're the Creator, we are the creation and sometimes, we just get that out of order. Forgive us. We trust You, Lord. We trust You with what looks impossible to man, remembering that all things are possible with God. Your grace is sufficient. In Jesus' name, Amen.

HIS EYE IS ON THE SPARROW

Children are a reward! Ah, some of you are scratching your head and saying, "You don't know my child! There's probably a poster out there with his picture on it saying "Wanted, Reward!" But my friends, the instant the words pierce the air in the delivery room announcing, "It's a boy!" or "It's a girl," an alarm sounds. Parents are placed on guard. That's right, God graciously allows and calls parents to a responsibility called "watch care." I don't know about y'all, but I took on that vocation with fear and trembling, coupled with the fierceness of a guard dog. Parenthood is one of the greatest mission fields.

For us, it became a foreign mission field and an adventure when we wound up with a child who brought with him many interesting twists and turns; you had to be a mental contortionist to keep up with his antics. I'm not kidding, our son Zach could preach on Sunday and be in the principal's office on Wednesday. We definitely had to keep an eye on him and a knee bent in prayer.

Have you found that when you expend yourself on those placed in your care, it's hard to relinquish the job? It's tough to cut the ol' umbilical cord. In fact, the knife felt pretty dull when Zach's calling became something other than we predicted. Observers said this kid had a propensity toward the following occupations: politician, used car salesman or preacher. He chose none of the aforementioned.

Never one to choose the easy, except when asked to do chores, it was one of those defining moments when Zach called us home to talk to some fellow sitting in OUR kitchen. There sat the greatest salesman on earth, The Marine Recruiter. Yep, he did it. Zach signed up to become one of the few, one of the proud, a United States Marine. This move took his dad and me by complete surprise. Zach felt the Lord was moving him to take this avenue. Lowry and I like to hear the Holy Spirit telling us the same thing when it comes to our child, but truth be known we weren't trying to listen. We liked having this guy around the house, or at least in the neighborhood. Uncle Sam wanted to move him to distant shores. We felt a definite rip in the ol' cord.

Slowly but surely, though, the day grew closer to the time when we'd have to wield the knife lest a ragged tear yield too much damage. It sure wasn't easy. Our boy would be moving to the other coast of the United States. I could hardly look at him without becoming a blubbering idiot.

Finally, sanity ruled and I focused on dealing with what was at hand. Zach could take a couple of things with him to boot camp: a religious medallion and money. Christmas was approaching so I decided to give him a cross to wear engraved with the word "Focus." If he was to be out of my care, then I sure wanted him to stay focused on his faith.

Every hour remaining with our son was precious, but I had committed a particular weekend to sharing my testimony with a group of women. When it came time for me to leave, I hugged my son. With tears in his eyes, he looked at me and out of the blue said, "Mom, I don't want that cross to say, "Focus," I want it to say "His eye is on the sparrow." This I could handle.

That weekend, I gave my testimony, which didn't include recent events; I just related my Savior's continued personal presence in my life. As I concluded and made my way to my seat, a young, beautiful woman from Louisiana came forward. I will never as long as I live, forget what happened next. Forever etched on my heart is the testimony to a personal intimacy of a loving God. Smiling sweetly she said, "God has told me to minister to you in song." That young woman who knew nothing of what was going on in my home stood before me and sang, "His Eye is on the Sparrow." That was a defining moment. God was standing watch. My duty was now complete. We had raised a child, I pray, to become a man who is independently dependent upon His Lord.

Zach has crossed an ocean, helped to set up a place called Camp Rhino, and is awaiting further orders as I write. I know whom I have believed and am persuaded that He is able to keep that which I have committed to Him against that day. His eye is on my Sparrow. You can know He is watching over your "reward" as well!

❀ ❀ ❀ ❀ ❀ ❀ ❀

Breaking ground, y'all – One of the toughest things many of us will ever do is to realize that our job is to raise our children to become INDEPENDENTLY DEPENDENT UPON GOD. But on that significant Saturday morning, the Savior's incredible gesture of love did more than that for me; it was a testimony to me that the Creator of the Universe knows each of us intimately, every hair or lack thereof. He knows YOU. I wish I was able to relate all the witnesses of others who have testified to that FACT.

Feel like you aren't one of those included? Please, get in a quiet place, seek the Father with all your heart, soul, mind and strength; trust His Word; listen for His voice; and even when you don't FEEL like you can hear Him—KNOW that His Word says His thoughts toward you are precious. All He asks is that you Believe in Him, Trust Him and be Obedient, regardless. HE IS ABLE!

Blossoms from The Book – Read Psalm 37! And then allow *Matthew 10:28-30* to speak to you: Do not be afraid of those who kill the body but cannot kill the soul. Rather, be afraid of the one who can destroy both soul and body in hell. Are not two sparrows sold for a penny? Yet not one of them will fall to the ground apart from the will of your Father. And even the very hairs of your head are all numbered. So don't be afraid; you are worth more than many sparrows.

Petals of Petition – Lord God in Heaven, thank You for the wonder of Your love toward each of us. Thank you for the precious gift of Your Son for the redemption of our lives, that while we were yet sinners, He died for us. That is too amazing to comprehend. Thank You that we can trust You with our children's lives; They are simply a gift from You. Father, in my own life I have realized that the wonder of it all is that You have given me the task to teach my children about You. That's where my assurance lies. They are Yours. We are Yours. When one of your precious sparrows wanders Lord, draw him or her to Yourself! Praise You. In Jesus' name, Amen.

GROUND BREAKIN'
MOMENTS OF YOUR DAY!

My husband got it right. Someone had said to my boss, "Do all these things really happen to Kandi?" To which he replied, "Yes, and more!" But Lowry said, "Kandi, these things happen to all of us. We just aren't always looking." So, it's my prayer that this humble little book has flipped the light on the landscape of your life, so you can see all the wonderful ways God is shining and filling your days.

I have specifically asked God to show Himself in the day. I wanted to be able to tell others about Him in the picture of life. He wants that for you, too. Look at your life today through the lens of faith! Take some time to write your story and see the Savior!

❀ ❀ ❀ ❀ ❀ ❀ ❀ ❀

❀ Tickle the earth with a hoe; it will laugh a harvest!

_____

_____

_____

_____

_____

_____

❀ One day I will burst my bud of calm and blossom into hysteria.

_____

_____

_____

_____

_____

_____

❀ ❀ ❀ ❀ ❀ ❀ ❀ ❀

While the earth remaineth, seedtime and harvest,
and cold and heat, and summer and winter, and day and
night shall not cease. Genesis 8:22

FERTILIZIN' FAITH MOMENTS

❀ Compost…because a rind is a terrible thing to waste.

_____

_____

_____

_____

_____

_____

❀ Feed your faith and your doubts will starve to death.

_____

_____

_____

_____

_____

_____

❀ ❀ ❀ ❀ ❀ ❀ ❀ ❀

The way you turn a molehill into a mountain…
just add a little dirt.

A PULLIN' WEEDS KIND OF DAY!

❀ The difference between a flower and a weed is a judgment.

_____

_____

_____

_____

_____

❀ Some days feel like they're a few plants short of a full flat!

_____

_____

_____

_____

_____

❀ ❀ ❀ ❀ ❀ ❀ ❀ ❀

The garden that only has weeds pulled from it – but never a seed sown in it – still has no crop come harvest time.

BLOSSOMS BURSTIN' THROUGH!

❀ The seed is hope; the flower is joy…

_____

_____

_____

_____

_____

_____

❀ Gardening – just another day at the plant…

_____

_____

_____

_____

_____

❀ ❀ ❀ ❀ ❀ ❀ ❀ ❀

The mighty oak tree was once a little nut that held its ground.

ABOUT THE AUTHOR

Kandi Anderson hosts "Morning Lite" on WAOY, American Family Radio. She is an inspirational speaker and and columnist for the Mississippi Gulf Coast Sun Herald.

Kandi, her husband Lowry and daughter Kasie make their home on the Mississippi Gulf Coast. The grandchildren and their parents reside too far away for Maw Maw Precious' liking!

For booking or to correspond: kandi@waoy.com or www.jjjasper.com ("Kandi's Korner")